BECOMING RESILIENT

Love, Loss, Abandoned, Forgive

BECOMING RESILIENT

Love, Loss, Abandoned, Forgive

Loving a Man
Losing him to Covid
Abandoned by his Family
Yet I Forgive

BALEEIA MINGGIA-BAKER

BECOMING RESILIENT: Love, Loss, Abandoned, Forgive

Becoming Resilient is a work of nonfiction. Names of certain individuals have been changed for their benefit.

Printed in the United States of America

First Printing 2023

Copyright © 2023 by Baleeia Minggia-Baker

ISBN: 979-8-9879905-0-6

All rights reserved. No part of this publication may be reproduced, distributed or transmitted in any form or by any means, including photocopying, recording or other electronic or mechanical methods, without the prior written permission of the publisher, except in the case of brief quotations embodied in critical reviews or certain other non-commercial uses permitted by copyright law.

All scripture is taken from online biblegateway.com or online bible with the version of scripture noted.

Original poetry by Baleeia Minggia

Formatted by Show Your Success

Cover Design by Oksana Kacheeva

Covid 19 information came from social media editorial news articles and facts.

Dedication

This book is dedicated to those most important in my life.
Jesus Christ, Gerry, Deborah & Tinisha

All that I am and all that I have I dedicate back to God who has made everything possible in my life. **Jesus**, He is my Lord and Savior, always first in my life.

This book is also dedicated to the memory of the one true love of my life **Gerry Baker**. You expected me to write a book, a few books, we just didn't know the first would revolve around you. Thank you for believing in and encouraging me to do things beyond my imagination. Even more, thank you for loving me to the end, the one thing I always even wanted from you.

And of course I dedicate to our amazing daughters **Deborah Baker** and **Tinisha Butler**, You have supported, encouraged and defended me all along the way. You give me joy beyond words allowing me space and time to flow freely in writing and creative expression. I'm so thankful to be your mother. I am even more overjoyed to be **Christian Jr.** and **Nova's** YaYa.

He restores my soul and He leads me to the paths of righteousness for

His name's sake. Psalm 23:3

My light is too bright for darkness to overtake me.

Baleeia Minggia-Baker

Table of Contents

Foreword by Phyllis M. Brathwaite Ix

Introduction 1

Letter To The Widow 5

Love 11

Loss 61

Abandoned 89

Forgive 119

Conclusion 135

Acknowledgements 141

Special Acknowledgements 143

VIP Sponsors 145

About the Author 147

Foreword
by Phyllis M. Brathwaite

Baleeia Minggia-Baker is a Holy Spirit-filled vessel, overflowing with God-given gifts and talents, which God allows her to use for the benefit and edification of others. I met her about 25 years ago at a dance ministry festival hosted by her church, my sister church. She and I were the dance ministry leaders at our respective churches; she was the founder and choreographer of the dance ministry, comprised of children and adults. She also danced with the group. I, on the other hand, choreographed and taught children only, and was a "behind the scenes" leader. Throughout the years, Baleeia would encourage me to come to the forefront and minister myself. In God's time, I did just that, leading, choreographing and dancing with a group of mostly older women, known as The Ladies of Praise.

Baleeia and I became friends, as often happens in adulthood, slowly, over time. We initially bonded over our love of worshiping and praising the Lord through dance movement, but the occasional lunch, workshop, Bible studies and retreats solidified the relationship to be one as sisters in Christ. We were both married, raising families and experiencing life as Christian women seeking to discern and live our God-given purpose. In time, conversations became of a more intimate nature: sharing concerns, challenges, disappointments, joys, hopes and dreams. Laughter, as well as tears, were shared – the emotional glue of friendship. Venting and praying reinforced the bond; there's nothing like a praying sister-friend to confide in to help navigate life's turbulent waters.

As Baleeia's confidant, she shared with me many of the events recorded in her work, **Becoming Resilient.** Emotionally transparent and vulnerable, she related hurtful family situations, divulged her search and need for love, acceptance, and fulfillment, and expounded on her love of her nuclear and extended family with husband Gerry. She spoke of her passion and difficulty to live as God's Girl when often it seemed that Satan was working overtime to destroy that girl through serious illness, familial conflict, loss, betrayal, and abandonment. I often found myself looking across the table at her and thinking, "How can she still be standing? Still moving purposefully forward? Able to forgive and love?" I Knew the answer: GOD.

In Becoming Resilient, Loving, Losing, Abandoned, Forgive, author Baleeia Minggia-Baker will treat you, the reader, like an old friend getting together for a cup of coffee or tea, to share her life's truths, challenges and victories. She illuminates how the love of God has propelled her through some of life's toughest scenarios, and hopes that maybe her faith story can inspire readers as they journey through their own life story.

Phyllis M. Brathwaite

Introduction

If you are expecting to read a story about true love, you have found it. If you think you are reading a widow's story of loss and grief, it's here. If you are wondering what it's like to be betrayed and abandoned, that is here too. And if you want to know how I got through all of it and still have enough love to forgive all that has happened, you have found the right book to read.

God has blessed me to live a life I've enjoyed. It wasn't perfect, no one's life is. But if I had to choose mine over another, I'd choose to live my life again. I did not have a happy childhood family life. There were happy moments I remember that I am very grateful for. I love my family very much. I was born into one of the most creatively gifted families I know in spite of its shortcomings. But overall, for me inside it was a sad life. I wanted more. I wanted a family that had more love than arguments.

The roots of my family are very spiritual, full of ministers and chefs. However, I did not grow up in what one would call a saved household that read the word or went to church religiously, though we believed in God. We went to church on holidays and I was sent to Sunday school. I grew up with some knowledge of Jesus but without true understanding. I got married young at 19, trying to fix my sin of having sex before I was married with someone

I thought knew more than I. Someone with a family like I wanted. I turned out to be wrong. The picture was not what it seemed. Though the situation was bad and filled with pain, the Lord I had no full knowledge of at the time, blessed me with a child during that marriage. The ending of that relationship was the beginning of my new life. I was led to Christ with full understanding of who He is, giving my life to Him, wanting to live my life for Him. I gave him the desires of my heart and He blessed me with what I longed for all my life, love and a family.

When Gerry came into my life my whole world changed. Most of my life I was searching. I watched friends go to school, climb up the corporate ladder in careers, obtain degrees in school and begin businesses. I was happy for them and knew there were things I could do, but nothing felt right. I always said "I don't know what I want to be when I grow up". This was my mantra even into adulthood. But then I met Gerry while I was working in corporate America, everything changed. With Gerry I discovered who I was and what I wanted to be. I am meant to be his wife, mother of his children and keeper of his home. I love being a woman, wife and mother. I had finally found what I had been searching for in my life.

Being his wife was not always easy. What made us work was we each needed what the other had. We were able to see beyond one another's faults to what we each needed to make us complete. Even our worst times would not end us, our roots in one another were so deep. We had

Introduction

love that was meant to be. A lot of people including members of my own family didn't like it and were jealous of what we had. I was told "get a life" often. The problem was, those telling me to "get a life" were the ones who had no life of their own. They were unhappy in the life they were living and resented me being happy in the simple life I had. But what happens when the love of your life dies? Everything that made my world whole on this earth was ripped from me.

Now a widow never imagining my life without Gerry I have to start my life all over again. This has not been an easy path. That's putting it in the mildest of terms. Grieving sucks. Grieving Gerry is so much worse than any of the things I dealt with growing up and through my first failed marriage. The aftermath was an even more tragic experience. Together, those things made me look harder into who I am in God and if I truly trust Him. In the beginning, I didn't have confidence things would work out. I didn't believe God knew or saw me. I felt I was left on my own, all alone. But I was wrong. God sees me. He knows me. He loves me. Through Him I have been able to come full circle from love, loss, being abandoned and learned to forgive to become the resilient woman I am called to be, God's girl.

You may be reading this because you have experienced some of the things revealed in my story. If so, I pray you find a sense of comfort and healing. There will be some things written about people that paints them in a less than positive light. Life is not always pretty but what is written is true. Some know only part of the story, not the complete tale. Here all is told, not to condemn or tear down. It is to bring awareness of wrong and right. It is told with the hope lives will change for the betterment of all. If you in any way resemble one of those less flattering people in this book, it is not too late to change. Each day given to wake up and take a breath is a new beginning, leaving the past in the shadows of dark forgetfulness.

I pray my story shows other widows, our lives though we have gone through a drastic change, has not ended. Being resilient through our grief gives us a rich new beginning. We are one of the chosen few who have experienced what real love is. Some never have, nor ever will experience this gift of love God has given us. It's something to cherish for the remainder of our lives. I pray my story helps you BECOME RESILIENT.

Letter To The Widow

Forgive me for addressing the woman with whom I relate.

My Dear Sister,

You have now joined the club for which no one wants to belong. First, I want to tell you that I am sorry for your loss and that you are not alone. Losing our spouse is the worst feeling we can experience. The sudden loss feels like the air has been sucked out of you, your mind goes blank and you desperately want it all to be a bad dream. But it's not. It is also not the end of your life though it may feel that way. God is not finished with you, in fact He has more for you to do. Your new life is beginning. For those who took care of an ailing spouse for a period of time, the pain of that last day you looked into their eyes was no easier to say goodbye. You remain for a purpose to live God's plan.

At the time of writing this book, my husband will be gone for three years. I received condolences from friends, his co-workers, church members and neighbors. They sent cards, food and money all expressing how much they cared for me and him. People sent books and quoted scripture about him being in a better place. As true as those words were and as much as I love the Lord, I didn't want to hear it at the time. The best comfort I received was from other widows, for me to feel free to feel whatever I was feeling at the time I was feeling it. I was free to burst into tears, scream, curse or anything else that allowed me to release all I was feeling inside. I didn't have to hold back or hold in my feelings until I got home by myself. They were right and it did help.

I learned something more. After the initial cards, calls and letters that were so overwhelming at one time, now became deathly silent leaving me alone. When Gerry died, his friends in particular went out of their way to let me know how much they cared about him and would be there for our family. That I should call on them FIRST, if I needed help. Yet, when the time of need came, their words came up empty. They were not to be found. So create for yourself a list with a good and reliable electrician, plumber, roofer, handyman and even a contractor when that time of need comes. Even worse, someone he called "friend" and more than likely tried to help, stole a photo Gerry took with President Obama our daughter was to receive. I quickly learned, his friends are not my friends leaving our family cold. I can only hope the person who stole the photograph gains a conscience with integrity to return the photo. Simply drop it in the mail.

In my case, the pandemic delayed some things understandably but it was me and our girls alone when it came time to go through his things, putting our lives back together. It's still just us in most cases with the exception of my friends. These are the friends I had prior to meeting my husband. And one or two I met after. My husband was the smartest man I knew. He could see through people and tried to teach me to not be so trusting. He tried to prepare me for people.

There may come a time when you feel that you are alone in the silence. Build yourself a support group to hold your arms up when you feel like you are falling. Make me the first on your list. Grief comes in waves, there is no time limit for grieving. You will be happy, energetic and full of excitement at one moment. The next a flood of memories and missing will overtake you. It is normal. I still am grieving, my tears haven't stopped. Those who love you will understand. Each emotion and stage of grief will give you greater strength to walk through the fire. There is purpose in our pain, there is joy where our tears have fallen. God has us even when we feel like He has forgotten us. Our wailing in our loss will become worship as we draw closer to Him making us worshipping widows with arms open for the blessings yet to come. Together we become winning widows as we become resilient through our loss.

Finally, because we are a widow, does not mean that is where we must remain. If you desire for and the Lord blesses you with new love in your life, embrace it without a quilt. Some of us may remain alone for the rest of our lives and be content. For myself at this moment of writing, my heart is full. My life is complete. Whatever your future holds, embrace it as you BECOME RESILIENT.

God's Girl

I Am A Lily

I come from a family of Mums
All different colors blooming to shine in their season
Each has lots of tiny petals formed around their center
However, I myself am not fond of being a Mum
I choose to be something different
I decided to make myself into a Calla Lily
A Calla Lily stands single with a narrow base
Then she slowly opens curving into a soft delicate shape
They laughed when I told them who I am
Their thinking was that I think I'm better than a Mum
It's not that, something inside just told me I'm meant to be different
I'm not meant to blend in, but to stand out, set apart from the group
Yet making that choice meant I must stand alone
It's a lonely place at times, but a peaceful one too
And that is what I do
There are bees that flood around my bloom with their sweet nectar
But once they find out no matter how sweet their buzz may be
My blossom is closed to just any bee, so they get bored and fly away
Alone I bloom for that chosen bee worthy of my release
Only then will a new garden of Calla Lilies bloom out of the roots of Mums.

Baleeia Minggia (2022)

Love

For this cause shall a man leave his father and mother, and cleave to his wife; and they twain shall be one flesh: so then they are no more twain but one flesh. What therefore God hath joined together let not man put asunder.
Mark 10:7-9 (KJV)

Before there was a television series called "Love At First Sight" or "Love Is Blind"; there was "How Gerry met Leeia." Our meeting was just as unconventional as either of these two popular television series. And just as exciting if you were watching from the outside. We met by telephone. Yes, that's right. I said we met by telephone, not seeing one another face to face until about a month or more later. All we had was a voice on the other end of the phone line.

Gerry was working for CCBSS downtown in Camden, New Jersey. I was working in Cherry Hill at the new corporate headquarters of SOA. It was early in the new year. Though I had sent a prayer to heaven three years earlier asking the Lord to send His choice into my life, which I know He heard and answered. He just wasn't answering quite fast enough for me to realize He was in the midst of answering it in my near future.

My life was in a good place. No, it was in a GREAT place. I lived in a beautiful two bedroom townhouse apartment I could afford, comfortable for KCJ and myself. My job at SOA was going well. I loved my church St. John's United Methodist Church in West Berlin, New Jersey, where Rev. Calvin R. Woods was the pastor. I had a good group of friends, with the best of all being my neighbor in the apartment next to me, Bernice. I loved my life with the Lord, but longed to be married and for my son to have a father in his life. His father, my ex, walked out before KCJ's second birthday and hadn't looked back. But this is not about him. The only thing missing was that one person to share my life with. I was meant to be a wife with a family to love and be loved by.

So, I sent up my prayer three years earlier in expectation and asked God to answer. And He did. I felt it in my spirit without a doubt. Only the manifestation of that prayer wasn't seen in the year or so I was looking for it to be answered. People ask how do you know when God speaks to you? It's hard to explain, but He does. Sometimes it's audible, other times it's a feeling inside you can't explain. You just know. This was one of those times. I felt His yes inside of me so deeply I began to weep. I also began to wait. God's time is not always on our time. Co-workers would try to fix me up on dates, all ending in disaster to the point I stopped thinking about "dating". It was all bad. I didn't realize I was trying to help God out in finding my person with the "help" of some well meaning friends. I should have been telling myself "God don't need no help,

Leeia". If I was going to trust him I should trust him and leave it alone. When I put my hands in it it was a mess. Every "date" I was fixed up with to go out was worse than the one before. The final straw was when the guy took me to the movie expecting to come back to my apartment for the night. We didn't even eat out. Nevermind I was in a one bedroom apartment with my son sleeping at the time. I'm not that girl. Of course he never came flat out saying his plan. First it was he was tired, wanting to lay down. I told him he could grab some coffee at the coffee shop in front of the complex to wake up. Then he thought we could have breakfast in the morning. I told him McDonalds was up the street on his way out. I was done and he was too. I never saw him again. Tyler Perry wrote, "I Can Do Bad By Myself". That's exactly how I was feeling. The last man I was with was my ex-husband. I'm not a side piece, a one night affair, a prude or anything else you want to call it. I just have higher standards giving my word to God I would wait on who He sent into my life. Because things didn't go in the way I thought they should, I stopped thinking about God's yes and gave up. I accepted I would be alone for the rest of my life, and that was ok with me. Things began getting so much better after accepting that.

Gerry was pretty much in the same place. He had gotten out of a relationship type situation, and in his words, he was ready to be single and free, enjoying his life without attachment. He was looking forward to having his summer parties, reflecting on his famous Virgo parties.

I didn't know him then. He liked his job at CCBSS and the people he worked with, along with it paid well. His rent was almost non-existent due to his renting out some space of the home he was renting. His parents used to live in the home but sold it. Now Gerry was renting from the new owner. Gerry was always a sharp business person finding the right deal. The female tenant he was not in a relationship with, primarily paid the rent required for her child and herself. This freed up his funds to raise full time his two children from a previous relationship. Having a female and her child afforded them both someone to look after the kids if one of them had to leave for a period. This worked out very well for him when he worked his part time overnight job on occasional weekends. His life was smooth and predictable.

We both were actively moving in our lives not making plans of meeting anyone. We were pretty much content with the flow of our individual lives doing things the way we want. That's when God made His move. I liked my position at work. I had been with the corporation just under five years and loved working there. Then my department got an additional new manager I was sectioned to work with. Our personalities didn't mix mostly I believe, because I was not personally interested in him beyond the work I had to do for him. I got along well with and enjoyed all other managers I worked for through the years without issue. I was having a difficult day at work dealing with him and called my friend and neighbor Bernice at her job to vent. She worked at CCBSS in the food stamp department with Gerry. She never talked much about her job. I didn't know they shared phones. When I called, Gerry answered on the other end. I asked to speak to Bernice. He told me she was away from the desk, but I could leave my number and he'd have her call me back. I didn't know this man from Adam and after dealing with those past date issues I didn't want to leave my phone number with an unknown man. They didn't have caller id back then. I quickly told him "I'll just call her back". I tried again at a later time ending with the same result, with Gerry answering the phone again. I was beginning to wonder if Bernice ever picked up the phone. By the third call he asked, "will you please leave your number, I promise to have her call you back?" This time I did, and she called me back.

When she got home that evening she came by my apartment and said to me "You know that guy who answered the phone?", "yeah" was my reply. She continued, "he was asking all kinds of questions about who you were, and said, he loved your voice". I told her, "oh really"? in a, I could care less, kinda way. Flashbacks of mr. I'm tired and hungry from my last apartment, crossed my mind. I told her "Oh no!". She then told me, he's a nice guy though she didn't get along with him. I told her, "That's nice, but I can do bad by myself". I didn't realize I was pushing away my blessing. I could almost see God smiling down at me. He was probably laughing too.

Another week went by where I was having an extremely rough day. This time I was in tears. Once again, I reached out and called Bernice. She actually answered the phone when I called. I was pouring out my heart to her of what I was going through when she told me to hold on. A moment later Gerry was on the phone. I hadn't said anything to him about the situation but as he began talking, he gave me a new perspective for what I was dealing with, and made me laugh. I was surprised by how at ease I felt in the short conversation. Then he asked, "Can I please meet you?" I was hesitant, I still wasn't dropping my guard completely, but said OK. After saying yes to meeting him, you'd think it would take place relatively soon, within a week maybe. That wasn't the case for us. Our meeting didn't happen right away. We spoke on the phone more frequently, becoming daily for weeks. He confessed he kept my phone number the day I finally gave it to him for Bernice to call me back. He said he wrote it on his desk calendar so he'd have it. I just shook my head. See, that's why I didn't want to give my number to a stranger. But in this case, I'm glad I did.

After all those weeks of talking on the phone day and night, we eventually set a time and place for our face-to-face meeting. Gerry was a very active member of his local union, CWA Local 1084, and they were sponsoring an event for Jim Florio, the governor elect at the time. The union sponsored an event to be held at the Hyatt Hotel in our area. Gerry invited me to the event where he was acting as the photographer for the union. He was editor of

Love   17

their local newsletter too. I had made it clear prior to our planning our face to face meeting I would drive myself wherever we first met and it had to be in a public place. This way, if things weren't right, I could get in my car and be gone.

Once we agreed to the meeting time and place, we each described what we would be wearing to identify one another. We already had vague descriptions of what we physically looked like. I was nervous meeting him for the first time. Since my divorce three years earlier there had been no man, I let get close to me the way Gerry was. With the exception of those few horrible fix ups that barely knew my name, and had no chance at getting close. I told Gerry I'd meet him there and described the dress with color it would be I was wearing. He was ok with that.

The description Bernice gave me of Gerry was him being of fair complexion with brown hair, nice looking, very vague. When I arrived at the hotel I entered the lobby taking a glance. I thought I had seen him but wasn't sure. The man I saw was extremely fair at a distance, could pass for white, and his hair was a light sandy brown. He was wearing a sweater with maroon in it matching the description of my dress color. When I saw no one else fitting the description I was originally given, I began looking around this noisy crowded space. Then I turned and we saw one another at the same time, he said "Leeia?" I responded "Gerry?", That's when we both smiled and said "hi" in person for the first time. It was nice to put face to voice after all this time.

Gerry was the perfect gentleman. The ballroom was packed with people. As we tried walking through, he asked if he could put his hand on my back guiding me through the people as he took photos. It was ok with me. I had a feeling of calm when I met him. He felt safe. I followed him as he took photos in this noisy space. A part of me was in awe with what he did and how well he was received by people. When he stopped taking photos he said we should find a spot where we could talk beyond the noise. He had come to the event with his former sister-in-law Martha who drove him there. He asked if I minded giving him a ride home so she could leave when she wanted. By this time, I felt pretty comfortable in his presence. I told him I would be glad to drop him off, but I don't want to get lost. I knew nothing about Camden, not even enough to be fearful of driving in Camden at night alone. I just had such a bad sense of direction where I could get lost in a paper bag. I once broke off my inside car door handle in a panic when I got lost. I forgot the door was locked when I tried to get out for help, to get back on the right track. I didn't want to experience that feeling again. He assured me he'd put me on the right path home. I would not get lost.

We found a spot to sit in the lobby. The hotel has an area a stone's throw away from the front desk. It was a sunken area on the lobby floor where you could sit and talk. As we sat, I noticed Gerry had a drink in one hand and was smoking a cigarette in the other. Both were turn offs for me even with him being such a nice guy. I thought about saying nothing at first, but then though, since this was our beginning with nothing invested, I saw no reason to not be honest. There was no point in wasting either of our time trying to impress one another if it was going nowhere. I have my car and can drive home. I'd still be nice enough to drop him off like I promised and would just not see him again. It sounds like a lot, and I was. That's what happens to women who have been through the wringer and put up walls. I still was not thinking about how the Lord told me "yes" three years earlier.

I told Gerry, "I don't like people who drink or smoke". His response was matter of fact with a slight smile on his face "this is as bad as it gets". I then told him "I have a five-year-old son and if you can't deal with him, you can't deal with me". Once again, without a blink, his response was "I'm raising two kids of my own, what else you got?" I looked at him almost surprised he hadn't gotten up to go. That would run most men away. But not Gerry. Finally, I told him "The next man in my bed is my husband, so if you're looking for sex that's not happening". He told me, "There are plenty of women around here to have sex with, if that's what I wanted. Is there anything else?" With that I exhaled and relaxed as we continued talking and laughing getting to know one another more for the rest of the evening.

I drove him close to his home. He wanted to assure me I would not be lost so he had me drop him off at the end of his block in the Parkside section of Camden where he lived. This way I could turn around and get back to the highway to return to my home in Pine Hill. Before he exited the car, he did something I wasn't expecting. He gave me the sweetest kiss on my right cheek as he said goodnight. He didn't attempt to approach or invade my personal space in any other way.

There was something about that kiss. It was an awakening I didn't understand. I had forgotten all about my prayer God responded to. At this moment, it felt like a light came on inside of me I didn't know how to perceive. I was also too afraid to think that maybe this could be something real. Gerry was just too nice. He was a man a few years older than me which usually made me uneasy. He was experienced with children and had so much going for him. Why was he single and never married after all this time? He was such a great guy. And what did he see in me?

Worth the Wait

About a year ago I think
Or maybe a little more
I sent my prayer to heaven
Hoping you'd come to my door

I said 'Father send someone
Who would fulfill all my needs
Communicate with understanding
Not treat me as they please'

Then I waited for what I thought
Was an extremely very long time
I said 'Father, what's taking so long?'
He said "It comes in only my time"

"So dear child please take your time
Place all faith and trust in me
When I allow the moment to arise
All will be as it ought to be"

Then at once when I least expected
From nowhere I heard your voice
May inner spirit touched my soul
Telling me, you are God's choice.

Baleeia Minggia (1989)

Love

We continued with this growing relationship of sorts. Neither of us jumped ship or ran away after that initial face to face meeting. Still we hadn't had what you would call an official date. Over time, we later had an actual date where he invited me out to dinner. It was at this time I learned he did not drive. I was a little surprised, but considering the man I met, and could feel myself falling for, I was not put off. It also never kept him from getting anywhere he wanted to go, including commuting back and forth from Camden to Glassboro State College. Now known as Rowan University. He took me to Walts, a seafood place in Philadelphia. Gerry had me take the Patco Train to Camden where he met me on the platform. It was unusual but it worked and he was worth meeting up that way. I had never been to Walts before so I didn't factor in the walk along those city blocks wearing heels. We talked along the way, taking our time and the food was delicious when we got there. It's the first time I actually saw and ate mussels. Gerry had a big bowl covered in garlic and loved them. We had a beautiful evening together. Each moment spent with him was better than the time before.

Our conversations increased. I learned he didn't drive due to his vision. Correction; he never had a license to drive legally and for the safety of himself and others he didn't anymore. That's not to say he didn't do it in his younger careless years. Anyway, as I was saying. He was not albino but carried the albinism trait giving him astigmatisms in both eyes for which he wore contacts and thick glasses. I could see his eyes shake. He had beautiful gray/green eyes hidden behind those rims. He had an exceptional eye doctor, Harvey Wolbransky who maintained his vision through the years seeking ways to make it better. Even knowing this, he never revealed how poor his vision was. He kept it hidden like his missing front tooth his brother knocked out when he was a kid. His confidence and strength to have the ability to do whatever he set his mind to made me admire him all the more. I was growing more comfortable in our conversations though I still had minor reservations. I take people at their word trusting until I am given a reason not to trust them. I at least took Gerry at his word. Gerry on the other hand can be a little less literal. Like most people. We were on the phone after work one evening and he had to take care of something. He told me he'd call me right back. I said ok. Then I waited, and waited, and waited. He didn't call back and it was time for bed. I got really annoyed he hadn't kept his word. I purposely waited until midnight when I knew he'd be asleep, then I called him. When he answered in a sleepy voice, I asked cheerfully, "did I wake you?" He responded "yeah". I told him "good, don't ever tell me you're going to call me back and don't do it, goodbye". Then I hung up the phone and went to sleep. I didn't care if he never called me back again. I'd rather be a little hurt now than a whole lot later. I didn't want to be his toy. He thought I was crazy, and maybe I was, a little. He also told me later, along with thinking I was nuts, he knew then he was going to marry me. I guess he was a little nuts too. Obviously he called me again, and he never told me he'd call and not do it.

Though Gerry grew greater in my life, I didn't let it waver me from who I was. I continued going to church every Sunday singing in the choir led by my friend and brother in Christ, Michael Troutman Sr. and attended bible study. My activities during the week remained the same, just as he did. We had our separate lives. We saw one another little during the work week even though we worked only a few miles apart. The weekends were our time to be together the most. I never pressured him to attend church with me though he knew it was a great part of my life. If he wanted to see me, he knew where I would be on Sunday. I wasn't mean about it or preachy with a halo over my head in prayer. I just knew what felt right for me, keeping me grounded. If he wanted to come he was welcome, otherwise he could see me after church. I asked him early in our relationship if he went to church. He told me he was saved, but in a "backsliding" state and he watched football on Sunday. I wasn't sure what the backsliding state was all about. I just knew he was respectable towards me and what I believed with no pressure for anything. How and who he represented himself to be prior to our meeting did not exist to me.

Eventually on his own he began taking the train from Camden to Lindenwold. He'd have me pick him up at the train station to come to church with me. That was God. It took effort for him to come because our service began late due to my pastor, who was over three churches at the time, had to come from preaching his first message at his church in Camden. By the time he got to Berlin, that was prime time with the football game on. It made me happy he desired to be there. I saw growth and change with even more things to talk about. In all that time, there was never pressure on him to join my church. I was simply happy he came to attend on his own. Seeing him in service was enough. We began sharing the word in discussions. Gerry was a history buff and liked talking about biblical history and prophecy. I liked reading Jesus' parables and miracles. We both studied the Proverbs as a way of living. We learned from one another and sometimes even competed about what we learned in our growth.

One Sunday while I sang with the choir, Pastor Woods as always gave the call to anyone who wanted to give their life to Christ and join the church. I wasn't paying attention at first sitting there in the choir loft. But then I looked up. That's when I saw Gerry was at the altar. I was overwhelmed. He not only recommitted his life to Christ but he also joined the church. That was a major step in our lives I had nothing to do with. It connected us on an even higher level than before. I couldn't ask for anything better. He later got baptized as well.

I didn't have a lot where finances were concerned. I was able to pay my bills with maybe a little extra. That was enough for me. Buying him a gift was not in the budget, but I wanted to give him something. I did the next best thing I knew how. I baked a carrot cake for him and his children. It was my way of showing I cared. He took it with a smile, never telling me he didn't like carrot cake.

However, a few days later the cake came up in conversation. I asked him how he liked it. That's when he told me he didn't like carrot cake but ate the whole thing. He said it was so good, he didn't even share it with his kids. That was a major compliment to me. He went on to say I should be selling them. Always the businessman. I told him I couldn't do that. I'm not a salesperson, but I was happy he enjoyed it. Around this time, he also gave me the nickname "Nikki". He never said exactly why. It was his pet name for me. The last pet name I was given was "squirrel" a long time ago. That's another story.

He listened to me as I juggled taking care of my bills since my ex skipped town rather than pay the mandated child support for KCJ. Gerry wanted to do more and more for me but I remained pretty independent not wanting to rely on him taking his money then feeling like I owed him. Having cable with HBO was the one extra thing I could afford. Having that meant I no longer had to rent movies from the video store. Then one month I was trying to figure out what I could juggle around to pay my auto insurance bill that was coming due. I didn't want to go to my mother either. She has helped me out before. Gerry offered to give me the money but I wouldn't take it. I then thought about the cake. I asked him if he really thought people would buy my cakes. He said sure, just give him some samples. I started baking right away, giving them to him the next day. When I gave the samples to him, I wasn't sure what would happen next. To my great surprise, he came back to me with orders for my cakes. I didn't know what to sell them for or anything else. I just baked. He set the price telling them if they were not happy, he'd give them their money back. The last part made me nervous. I needed that money for my insurance payment. Nevertheless, I never had to return anyone's money. They just kept ordering more. He truly had the gift of gab and a great marketing sales person.

I'd sit up at night after work baking then I would drive the cakes to Camden giving them to him. He took them on the bus with him to work to sell. He then brought the money back to me. I made enough money in two weeks to cover my insurance bill. I couldn't believe it. There were people who ordered cakes every payday. He came up with the name Nikki B's for the cakes after his pet name for me. The B represented both my first name and his last. In the beginning the packaging was rough. They were baked in a foil pan with aluminum foil on top. He told me the cakes were good and sold themselves. Now we needed to look at the presentation of my cakes. I took it all in and made positive changes making things that much better. Gerry inspired me to do and be more. He gave me confidence I didn't have before. I trusted him completely, and that said a lot for me coming from a place that neither trusted nor felt safe with men.

I began helping Gerry with the union newsletter too. I typed the pages for him as he did the layout for the paper. He taught me how not to use too many fonts, making reading easy. He also made sure the page was not too busy. Any time we could spend together was a good time, be it work or play. We began to confuse people too, not intentionally. But it was fun. Sometimes Gerry would call me Leeia, other times he called me by the nickname "Nikki" he gave me. When I'd call him at the office, sometimes I'd say it was Nikki, other times Leeia. Then there were times I'd just ask to speak with Gerry. Whoever would answer would tell him they didn't know if it was Leeia or Nikki thinking he was involved with two different women. That must have been Gerry prior to me, not realizing I was one in the same. He'd chuckle as he told me about it, keeping a bad boy image. None of them knew the Gerry he became when we got together. The silly and romantic one, even vulnerable at times with me. I guess he felt safe to be himself too. Gerry even stopped smoking, at least when I came around at first. I didn't have any hassle with him about it. He knew I didn't like it around me. I never mentioned anything about his smoking after that first evening we met, though my face may have. Gerry was just respectful of my feelings. One day when I was walking up to his building to see him, he was standing outside with a friend having a cigarette. At first he didn't see me, but then he recognized my walk. I watched him as he threw the cigarette on the ground behind him. I thought it was cute. Almost like a kid getting busted by his mom. I met him with a smile and told him I saw what he did, then laughed. It meant so much he cared that much about what I thought. How could I not love this man?

The weather was getting warmer and we looked forward to hanging out in little outings. The Berlin Farmers Market was one of those hang outs. Gerry enjoyed buying me outfits to wear. I would let him do that. He bought me a set that has a striped top and a short red skirt with suspenders. I guess it was somewhere in June and he wanted to introduce me to his parents. They were having a small family cookout, nothing special. We drove to his parents home in the Whitman Park section of Camden. His older brother Roman called as we were on our way so we picked him up near the train station. Roman was caramel around the same height as Gerry. He was nice looking with a little swag and smiled when he met me saying "hi" when Gerry introduced me.

We got to their parents where his dad was sitting out back near the grill. Mister is tall and bald, the color of milk duds. He appeared to be the serious type but gave a grin when Gerry introduced me as his girlfriend. His mother, who was very fair like Gerry but not quite as light. She had short brown hair and was pleasant. However, she was apprehensive about me. Gerry was her one son who had never been married, nor close to it, dating a divorcee with a child. She also liked the girl he was kind of seeing the prior year. Gerry saw that relationship as nothing serious, though the girl wanted it to be more; until he ended it. His father just chuckled seeing Gerry with this skinny girl in the short skirt he bought me. I began feeling a little uncomfortable in this skirt shorter than I was used to wearing. I chatted with Mister in the

Love

backyard as Gerry talked with his mother. Though brief, overall it was a nice day meeting half his family.

I met his younger brother Dale and his fiance Rosa at a later time, on their wedding day. Gerry invited me to attend with him. I purchased glasses as a gift from us both. I'm glad I did, he hadn't thought of buying a gift. Dale was kind of tall, dark chocolate with a square head and big smile. Rosa, was a thin white girl at the time with dark hair. They got married in his grandfather's house and reception in some small building afterwards. We didn't have communication with the exception of hi and congratulations. It was their day dressed up in pink and white. Their oldest brother Samuel wasn't there. I hadn't met him yet. I think he might have been away on "vacation" at the time. Gerry and I only saw one another and had not yet known what would transpire a year from now, from just one phone call.

Our relationship progressed to the point we both knew it was not a passing phase. We looked for ways to spend even more time together whenever we could. We'd take spontaneous trips on the train to Atlantic City just to walk and talk along the boardwalk together holding hands laughing. He was always one to take pictures so we took silly ones together. We even took a picture at one of those old time booths on the boardwalk where I dressed like a saloon girl holding a bottle of whiskey and him a bandit. We didn't end the boardwalk trip until he'd gotten a gyro from "Bill's" . The place has dollar bills with writing taped on every spot from ceiling to floor from customers who left their mark on a bill that they were there. We did too. Then we'd walk back to take the train home. Together we were in our own world. It was nice. But we knew there was more than us to think about. I wasn't spending as much time with Bernice as before. If it weren't for her, we'd never have met. She was happy for me and involved with developing her Mary Kay business.

As much as we loved our times together, we were very different. Gerry loves sports. When we weren't off somewhere together, he was coaching a team for Whitman Park Little League. He was a Philadelphia fan to heart regardless of sport football, baseball, basketball, even a little hockey. However, the PHILADELPHIA EAGLES topped the list. When other people got mad at their losses and began supporting other teams, he hung in there with the Eagles. He had all the faith in the world in his Eagles. Dallas Cowboys, the Eagles rival, had to be his least favorite team. He could not see how you could be from this area and root for a team in Texas. Those were always good games for him. He has more Eagle hats than I've seen. Every time a new Eagle hat came out, he got it. And he would not part with any one of the old ones. Gerry believed one day they would win the Superbowl. It didn't matter who laughed at his belief. He was a Philly Eagles fan 1000% through and through.

Gerry enjoyed a good fight too. I am not a sports enthusiast at all. I get the basics of most sports. They just don't excite me in the way it does those who follow them. I was a cheerleader in high school and a flag girl marching with the band at football games, but I just didn't latch onto sports like some others. I suppose I'm too practical to understand the noise of yelling at a team or television when they can't hear you anyway. Nor why people get so upset afterwards if it's a bad call or they lose. It's just a game increasing anxiety as I see it, even if it is not to them. Still, I respect the sportsmen's appreciation for the sport just as I have an appreciation for creative arts and theater.

Camden did not have HBO in Gerry's area at the onset of some of the Tyson fights. There was a fight in July of that year, Tyson vs Carl Williams. I didn't really care about the fight, real life violence did not appeal to me. Even in a controlled arena. He wanted to see it though, so I let Gerry have friends come to my place to watch it on HBO. He paid to have the fight plugged in and watch with his friends. They each paid their share back to Gerry I'm sure. When he came, I'd go and stay upstairs in my bedroom sewing or doing something else. He let them in as they came, however many there were. I could hear them while they hollered and enjoyed themselves. I never noticed who came, it was his night and space for the evening. Before he left to go home, he thanked me with a big hug and kiss, making sure everything was as neat as it was when they came. I think he appreciated that I wasn't one of those girlfriends who had to be in the middle of the game with his friends. I never asked any questions about anything that went on during that time. It was boys' night and I gave him his space.

We hung back for a little while prior to introducing our children into the relationship. Even though things were going pretty great, you never know where things are going to go. We didn't want our kids involved unnecessarily. Our relationship was moving quickly. Much quicker than either of us expected seeing that we were only together for a few months. We didn't want to spend a day apart and knew it. He told me he loved me first. I felt the same way but was afraid to say it. I would tell him "I like you a lot". He told me he loved me all the time with a point of letting me know, he never told anyone he loved them this much. Eventually I couldn't hold out any longer. I told him I loved him too. I loved him more deeply than he could ever know. I didn't want to be without him. It was now time to meet the kids taking the next step. The "I like you a lot" became a standing joke for us.

My son KCJ being young was an easy attachment. He was a small ball of energy used to being an only child but wanting a dad and siblings. Gerry had a son and daughter, Israel and Egypt. I was really excited about him having a daughter. I was looking forward to meeting Egypt. I always wanted a daughter to do things and hang out with. His children were very different though. They were older, fourteen and twelve, not as receptive as my five-year-old. Egypt, the oldest at fourteen was a cute light brown skinned girl, with thick hair and a pretty face with a mole above her lip. She pulled her daddy's heart strings. Israel was a little on the heavy side, light brown, cute face and mischievous smile. He followed in Egypt's shadow trying to be what his dad wanted.

Gerry tried to see how we could get the kids together by watching KCJ for me when I worked my second job at the Cherry Hill Mall, rather than me paying a babysitter. He'd give my KCJ dinner with his kids while keeping him at his house. I'd pick him up after work, then drive home. It seemed to work out pretty well. KCJ liked spending time with Gerry and usually fell asleep on the way home. I only had to put him to bed. My interaction with his kids was limited in passing. I never really spent time with them. They were either doing something else or not there when I came by since I primarily spent time with Gerry on weekends when they were with their mother. During the week, it was a quick hi, how are you then they were off, and I was out the door headed home.

Once we thought it was safe, Gerry and I began to talk about marriage. I was excited. I was really going to be married again. This time for all the right reasons in the right way. My prayer was being answered. Then my impatience started weighing in. I was beginning to have doubts. Gerry said he wanted to marry me but he still hasn't given me a ring. Things hadn't changed between us. We were just as close as ever before. There was no reason to doubt him. It was just my own insecurity and lack of belief someone this wonderful was going to marry me.

On one particular night in October I went to Gerry's. He was frying chicken. He loved chicken and fried it a lot. I used to tell him, he was going to start clucking soon. He had a way of putting a cut onion in the center of the pan of hot oil while frying for flavor. I never saw that before, but was impressed to see a man cooking in the kitchen for his kids, and for me for that matter. I sat on a stool in the corner of his kitchen sulking about not having a ring. All of a sudden, that's when he turned around to me with a ring in his hand and said "BAM!, marry me". I was shocked and laughed, we both laughed having a proposal over fried chicken. Something we never would forget. I loved how he was able to do that. It wasn't set up in a romantic setting of roses or a harp playing. Gerry being Gerry was more than enough, however he did it. I just wanted to feel his love. That's what made things so memorable. He was trying to wait to give me a bigger ring, but I was impatient. For me the size of the stone didn't matter. It wasn't even so much about getting the ring either, though I complained. I just wanted to know I was his and the world to know, he was mine. That night I received his ring and a unique marriage proposal to go with it, matching our meeting one another over the phone. It's a story we'd tell our grandchildren.

We could now share with our families the good news we had already known for some time. That didn't turn out exactly as we imagined. Of course, KCJ was happy. He was finally getting a real dad in his life. However, when Gerry told his kids we were getting married they thought it was a big joke. They did not believe him, they laughed. Egypt hoped it was a joke, because she didn't find it funny at all by the look on her face. They didn't think their dad would ever get married. Egypt surely did not embrace the idea of her dad getting married. She was the primary girl in his life all her life, not wanting to share him with any female on a permanent basis. Her actions quickly became very clear of how she felt about me. His son really didn't care. He almost wanted to express being happy, but not with Egypt standing near. He followed the actions of his older sister.

I thought Gerry's children's reaction was not good, but somewhat understandable as children. What I did not expect was the reaction of his parents when we gave the news. When Gerry told them we were getting married his father burst into laughter loud and hard like it was a big joke. He made some off the wall comments as if "who would marry you" though he may not have said those exact words. I looked at Gerry, seeing the hurt in his eyes, my heart melted. Sweety popped Mister on the arm to stop making a joke of it. She was somewhat surprised without adding much in a congratulatory manner. I asked him why his father would act like that. He brushed it off saying it was because he never told them he was getting married before. I didn't know how to take that. His brothers have all gotten married or were in a common law marriage. Why would they not expect the same for Gerry? It really was a downer. Even more, I felt the need to look out for and guard Gerry's heart. It didn't hinder us though. We planned to continue forward with our plans whether they were pleased or not.

I didn't introduce Gerry to my family in the beginning. He met them once before we became engaged. I was nervous for that meeting, telling him all about my family on the way to my mothers home in Beverly. I love my family, but I know we operate in our own dysfunction. Always cordial to outsiders, but as you get into the family you'll see the strong personalities that did not always get along with one another. This included loud opinions, arguments and long silences. Getting married early got me away from it, I thought. I don't like arguments or shouting so I stayed away from family gatherings except for my mother's birthday. We always celebrated her July 20th birthday with a cookout. I was thankful he didn't run off or judge me by their lives. Also that he saw me as separate from some of their actions. He saw me as an individual just as I saw him. My family's reaction to our engagement announcement was kind of mixed, but more positive. It would be my second time getting married. My family liked Gerry. Only one sister had something negative to say behind our back. She told our absent father I was marrying some "street N" from Camden. Yet, she was one of the first at our house on our wedding day. I only found out what she had said some years later. She had no clue who Gerry was, his education, ethics or work background. Some people just don't want to see you happy, even in your family. I'm glad everyone else liked Gerry.

We were planning how our future would be only to have all our excitement somewhat drained by our families. It would have meant a great deal to Gerry for his daughter and I to get along. I wanted us to get along too. I liked her and wanted her to like me. I always wanted a daughter, but I also had no clue on how to get through to a teen or raise one. We were just fifteen years apart. I tried as best I could to build a dialog with her, but she wouldn't even talk to me. I wasn't trying to take him away from her or be her mother. She had her own. I respected that. I just wanted to be another adult she could relate to. The problem was, neither of us knew how to relate to one another. The tension was so tight with her dislike of me being in Gerry's life to the point I felt a marriage wouldn't work. I hated the thought. It was breaking my heart because I waited for this. How could I marry a man whose kids, at least his daughter, hates me?

Feeling her deep bitterness towards me was too much for me to take. It was hurting me, and it was hurting him. I wanted it to stop. I called Gerry one night. It was a rainy night, dark and stormy, that matched my mood for what I was about to tell him. He asked what was wrong. I told him I loved him but if his daughter felt the way she did about us, our relationship wouldn't work. We would be butting heads and everyone would be miserable. I didn't want him to end up hating me or causing division between him and his daughter. We should just end the relationship for now and not get married. If it's meant to be, maybe when his kids have grown up some we can come together again if it's really meant to be. He refused to hear it, wanting me to drive to Camden to talk with him so he could convince me otherwise. I refused telling him it's best to leave things here. I was not coming to Camden. He then told me he was coming over to my home. I didn't believe him telling him, it's late and the weather is bad, let's just end things. He was insistent. When he makes up his mind to do something nothing stops him. I didn't believe him.

About thirty minutes later my doorbell rang. Gerry was at the door. He'd taken the train and a cab in the storm to my apartment. He was drenched, I couldn't believe it. I wasn't ready to see him. He came inside and I sat on the bottom of the steps that led upstairs. As hard as it was for me to say, I repeated everything I told him on the phone as he came and sat beside me. For the first time I saw tears in his eyes. He said, "Please marry me, I deserve to be happy". It made me cry. I love this man with all my heart and I finally found happiness. I deserved to be happy too. His is everything I asked God for, plus far more than I ever expected ready to push him away. I couldn't do it and wouldn't. I decided to marry him and stick by him no matter what or who came our way. He is worth it. Nothing was going to take away what we had finally found together.

My biological father was not in my life growing up. It was my mom, Aunt Elaine and my siblings. Gerry is the first real man and only man to show me what love really was.

He told me there are some women you date and others you marry. He told me, when he met me, he knew I was the marrying kind. That was the nicest thing anyone ever said to me. He also told me when he read Proverbs 31 it described me. That is an honor to be compared to her. In general, Gerry was not a romantic, but he had the most romantic moments and picked cards that told what was deep in his heart no one else ever knew. As we grew together, I could read his heart through the reflection in his eyes. The more I learned about Gerry and his life the more he mattered to me. I grew very protective of him, determined not to let anybody hurt him. I will fight for Gerry, when I have never, would never and it's debatable if I will ever fight for any man.

I couldn't wait to tell Bernice about our engagement. We talked about dates for the wedding and what it would look like depending on how soon we wanted the wedding to be. We talked about Valentine's Day with red and white or Christmas. Talking with Gerry we thought against it. It was too cliche and we didn't want our wedding to compete with a holiday. February was too soon and December was too far. I was expecting Bernice of course to be a part of our wedding party. She had to be my maid of honor. She is the reason all this is happening. Gerry and I continued to play with what would be a good wedding date giving time to plan, along with where we would live. My apartment was in a better school district but would have been tight for all of us to live in with three children. The kids, especially his daughter Egypt, were struggling enough just because she didn't want us getting married. As much as I loved my place, I didn't want to compound the situation with moving out of her environment. Gerry is renting a four bedroom house that has a fireplace. It was big enough but needed work, a lot of it. The problem was the owner didn't want to sell it to us, for us to make the investment in the repairs. This being the case, we decided to look for a home of our own to buy.

We decided to pick a date in June. It was a beautiful month and a different month from my prior marriage. The last day in June; June 30th we would become husband and wife. There was not a lot of time for planning. I immediately began looking for things for the wedding. Bernice was great at this. She knew how to shop for bargains. I had so much going on all at the same time, wedding and house hunting along with what has become my day to day life, work, cakes, church, and sewing. Somewhere in all of this time after the wedding date was set and we began looking for our home Bernice was gone. She left the job and had moved. It's like God placed her right where He needed her to be for me to meet Gerry and secure the relationship for marriage. I say this because six months prior to me moving next door to Bernice another apartment was available, but I was not ready to move in. Since I wasn't ready I had to go back on the waitlist. The next apartment to come up was the one next door to Bernice. Only now she's gone and I don't know how to reach her to be in or be at our wedding. That was my one disappointment of the day not having her at my side.

Gerry made a great income, but his credit was not so good. When looking for a home it was better to find a home I could afford since my credit was in good shape and I had a small down payment from an auto accident settlement. We looked at a few homes outside Camden, but they were not good for us and pricey. Finally, we saw a listing for our home in the Parkside section of Camden. I knew nothing about Camden with the exception of dropping things off to Gerry. He was born and raised here. He was shocked there was a home for sale on the street we chose. He said that this street never has anything for sale, it's a closed block on one of the nicest blocks in the city. Again, that was by God's design. I had written a poem, years earlier, maybe around the same time as my prayer about my dream house. And we found it, as close to the house I wrote about as we could get to it.

My Dream House

My dream house is not large,
but comfortable and small
Maybe three rooms, a fireplace,
A picket fence surrounding all

Inside is laughter, overwhelming love
Stern protection, plenty care
Warm nights, cuddling too
As we relax in an easy chair

We're well looked after, by He
Who holds it firm within his hands
Stands by us faithfully, watching over
You see He's God not a man

At night I kneel to say my prayers
In our quiet room all alone
Thanking for blessings and protecting
My dream house which is really a home.

Baleeia Minggia (1988)

The only problem was we were making a settlement on our new home in February, four months before our wedding. Gerry didn't want me to move into the house alone. He was concerned with me, a naive trusting single suburban girl moving alone to Camden knowing nothing about my environment. On the practical side, my lease was ending and if we moved in together, we could save money for the wedding. But I never shacked up, lived together with a man I wasn't married to. My faith wouldn't allow me. God's word is not to live in fornication, and I feared God. He had answered my prayers and living together would go against His word. I wasn't sure what to do, I know I didn't want to lose my blessings. We talked about it for a long time and wondered if we could live under the same roof until marriage and not have sex. We hadn't been perfect in our time together though we tried. Can we really stay together and not drink the wine when we have already had a taste of it? We were determined to try.

I am thankful Gerry is a man of God. We moved our two homes into one after we settled on the house. Some may not believe it, especially those who knew the old Gerry. But we moved into the house together and we did not have sex before our wedding. When I was weak, he was strong. And when he was weak, I was strong. It was only by God's grace we were not weak at the same time. June could not come soon enough resulting in the conception of our first born on our honeymoon, but that is later.

Our wedding day was the happiest day of my life. I was nervous too. I was happy to have my mother, aunt Elaine and siblings with me. They always showed up for the good things in my life with support, even if we weren't in a good place all the time. Their love was real, we just had difficulty showing it at times. There is nothing like family support. I expected it to be automatic with him because he did not come from a broken home as I did. When our day came I noticed the only members of Gerry's family who were at our wedding were his parents. His grandfather may have been there, I don't recall. I do know none of his brothers showed up. There was no card, they gave no gift congratulating Gerry. I came to know later that this has been the pattern in his family at least where Gerry was concerned. No one was there when he graduated from high school including his parents who went out of town so Gerry didn't show up to walk. Gerry graduated on the Dean's list from college and again, none of his family were showing up for him so he didn't walk. During the highlights of his life, he stood alone without his family. That was not going to happen anymore. I plan to always be there for him, he's worth it. He did have many friends and co-workers who showed up to fill the void which was a good thing.

Our wedding went smoothly. Even though Egypt wasn't happy about the wedding, she tolerated it well. She was pleasant and it was beautiful, everything I ever wanted. It was a real family affair too. My son walked me down the aisle. As we stood before Pastor Woods and he asked "who gives this woman?". In his small now six year old voice said "I do". Everyone chuckled while Gerry and I joined hands. In all my planning and preparation, I forgot the topping for our wedding cake. Thankfully a good friend found out before the service ended. He purchased one and had it placed on the cake prior to our arrival at the reception hall. We had a blast. In the end it was Egypt who caught the bouquet, and his son Israel caught the garter. We danced the electric slide and had a soul train line to die for. Mister cut loose doing the slop and Sweety looked gorgeous as ever. Maybe now that we are married things will only get better. We left the reception in our limousine for the weekend. We couldn't go away for a honeymoon at this time and we were both ok with that. We had each other.

We began our marriage with high hopes. At least I live in perpetual hope. It is not easy to blend two families into one with children who do not want you in their family. We went from starting out as a family of five. We quickly grew to seven and even eight for a time in a two year span. This was after Gerry, and I had two babies and took in Roman's son for a few years. Egypt didn't like the structure of our home, and of course she hated me. She didn't like that we all had chores and we ate dinner together as a family. We went to church together too. There was no choice not to go. If chores were not done privileges were lost. This is before technology really took over. The only thing she had was a phone in her room. A landline, that's all there was back then. If we took her phone, she'd bring home another one thinking she outsmarted us. I was pregnant at the time with our first child. Egypt and I were barely getting along and just had a big blow up a few days earlier. She decided she had enough and it would be better living with her mother. Gerry had just given her money to go shopping at the mall for her birthday. The following day, I was in the kitchen when I heard her come in the door from school. I called her name with no response. Then I heard her run upstairs to her room. She came down and went out the door again. I left the kitchen and went to the front door to find out what was going on. I saw her walking down the street with the bag of clothes she bought the day before. I kept calling out her name which she ignored. I didn't know what was going on. I called Gerry letting him know what had happened. It turns out she went to her moms deciding to not come back. It was to Gerry's disappointment, but he was growing tired of the tension. This didn't make it any easier. He tried to talk with her about it but finally let her go. When I gave birth to our first daughter Egypt came by the house to see what she looked like and left again. She still hadn't returned to our home and Gerry's annoyance had reached its limit. He didn't try to get her to come back. He let her be. He knew he did his best.

Much to my shock, I became pregnant again not expecting to be so soon. Gerry hadn't said much about Egypt whose birthday was approaching. I asked him if he was sending her a card or gift. He said no. I know that was not like him. He was hurt and I was afraid of this kind of division with us getting married. I wanted to help her to not feel like she was forgotten. So I got and mailed a card to her from her dad and myself. What I did not expect was the response. She mailed the card back to me torn up into little pieces and wrote a letter saying I was stupid having babies, that Gerry and my girls were bastards and threatened me to watch my back because I never know what will happen. I immediately showed it to Gerry while bursting into tears. Why would she attack me in such a way? Gerry was calm on the outside. I don't know what he ever said to her about it. He was not happy about it at all though. At that point I just stopped trying to do anything more for her beyond anything Gerry might ask.

Once Egypt was gone things in the house ran a little smoother though still very busy. We ended up taking in Roman's son Jacob through the foster care system. He was very helpful even with the problems he had faced. He liked living with us due to the stability we brought to his life treating him as an equal as all our children. To me he was our son. I felt pressure of working, taking care of two babies, going over homework, keeping the house, preparing meals and keeping the peace. While Gerry had it easy going to work coming home, changing then going out to coach little league. To this he went to his union's district meeting out of state, usually Washington, DC for a week during the year. Many times he missed dinner so I'd leave it in the oven and go to bed. We got up in the morning. I got in the car driving one way to work while he went in the other direction to work. We fulfilled our day's events only to see one another when we went back to bed at night. We were becoming two people cohabitating with the non-existent conversation about Egypt. That's not what I expected when we got married. I was beginning to feel like I was alone in the marriage after we began so great. We both forgot how to clearly communicate what and how we were feeling like we did in the beginning of our union. I wrote in my journal as I'd been doing for years telling God how I felt. God heard. He heard all too well and I'm thankful I didn't think or write anything more than I did. My words were precise enough. Perhaps too precise.

I became critically ill with toxic shock syndrome five years into our marriage and was hospitalized out of state in North Carolina. Gerry received a phone call at home in Camden with our girls who were only three and four years old, that I would be dead before he could get to me. I had taken the train there leaving our vehicle home. A good family friend Della told Gerry she'd drive him down there to me. Sweety came along for the ride to be with her son. They arrived on my 34th birthday not recognizing me at first. Gerry collapsed to the floor when he saw me. My body was swollen like a drowned victim due to all the fluids of medication being pumped through my body keeping me alive. He was devastated and inconsolable at times. Thankfully God was holding me in His arms and I remained. During the time I was away there were some issues going on with Israel causing him to leave our home permanently. Jacob returned to his dad some time earlier and was no longer with us. Gerry was left taking care of KCJ, Deborah and our second daughter Tinisha. I wasn't expected to live. I spent three months in a medically induced coma on a respirator. I had over a dozen chest tubes, and developed ARDS, leaving me with chronic bullous disease and fifty percent lung capacity. Yet God is so good and gracious, doing the impossible. It was while lying in the hospital bed he let me know He knew every part of me as reflected back in Psalm 139. He spared my life and I told Him I would do whatever He wanted from me. However, I wasn't aware of the assignment He had for me when I got home. Becoming permanently disabled at 34 was not my plan in life. I was always active, independent working two jobs. Now I don't work at all. I am a full-time wife and mother, which is not a bad thing. It was just a new thing to me. I didn't know this was who I was created to be. If I had to do it all over again, I'd jump at it. I love being a wife and mom. I also had more time for Gerry's parents when they called. It took this disability for me to learn this. The thorn in my flesh.

Sweety and I grew closer after having many talks. We began to form a special bond with open honest conversation. She would say we spoiled the kids a lot. We just saw it as loving our kids and giving them what we felt we were missing growing up. Pretty much like most parents. Being a full time wife allowed me to plan for more family gatherings. During the summer I would plan for cookouts with all the fixings. I didn't grill myself after my first and only disaster, setting the grill on fire. I left cooking the meats and anything else on the grill for Gerry. I only did prep for him. Around this time I noticed Mister had a habit of finding humor at another's expense. At the Mason banquets we attended for him he found humor in criticizing different people, the way they did things or calling them a big dummy like he was Fred Sanford. Then laughing loud and hard like he did when we said we were getting married, encouraging those around him to laugh too. In this case Gerry was the headline for his humor. The first time, everyone kind of laughed and blew it off. I think I first heard it at Mister and Sweety's house for something they were having. But later I noticed he'd say the same thing with every major gathering we planned.

Mister waited until he had everyone's attention then talked about Gerry as a child, how he used to shiver so bad while eating ice cream. Sweety would say how his lips would turn blue and his teeth chatter. But Mister would continue with "he talked in this squeaky high pitched voice. I thought he was going to be a fagot." Then he'd laugh long and hard. Please forgive me for even writing that word. I don't use it, I don't like it. In fact I HATE it and would never put it in reference to someone I love much less anyone else. Looking at Gerry I could see he didn't like and was embarrassed by his father always doing this. But we grew up in the era where you showed your parents respect and never said anything, even if they were wrong. When the girls were young and lacked understanding he tolerated it. But as they got older Gerry discouraged me from having gatherings with his family that included a platform for his father to talk about him this way. This I believe was the primary reason. Gerry had the need to make it plain he was a man and the only real man the girls and I ever knew. This in my thought was because of the degradation of his father, the man he was supposed to look up to. Yet and still, Gerry remained a constant help to and for his father trying to win his respect and approval. Much like all the boys.

I saw Sweety as a second mom. She shared several personal things with me, often advising me on things and shared recipes. My own mother and I were not always close. She saw me as the daughter she wanted, and treated me that way. I went to church on occasion with Sweety, I attended mother daughter luncheons with her at her church too. I even danced at one. Of course there were those gatherings for cookouts, until Gerry had me discontinue. We shared Thanksgiving and Christmas with them each year exchanging gifts. I cooked for them and learned some of Sweety's recipes Gerry liked, banana pudding from scratch, her baked beans and tuna noodle casserole. Mister entrusted me to plan and prepare her 80th surprise birthday party contacting her family she hadn't seen in years. It turned out beautiful and she thanked me with a beautiful letter calling me her daughter and how happy she was that I was part of her family. Most of all I took care of raising their grandchildren they were proud of without being a loud distraction. In short, I was the polar opposite of their other two daughter-in-laws. This also made those daughter-in-laws dislike me.

Surviving toxic shock syndrome with the capacity of one lung was a great miracle blessing from God. Leave it to the Lord to do and require the impossible. The Lord made me a worshiper telling me to dance for Him. It started small. A friend, Phil, I call my big brother, and a member of our church is a music producer who was working with a local Christian artist. His wife, Louise and I are good friends and she thought I could help working with him for his music label. It was a gospel CD. In the studio I began to see the music move while the musicians were laying down the instrumental tracks. From then God started downloading movement to me. It felt both strange and comfortable at first. I taught our girls who were now about five and six how to worship, teaching them the movement I saw in my mind.

What began with our girls spread to a few more girls, our pastors' kids. Over time, that grew into a dance ministry of about 30 people. I didn't dance at first. I'd never had dance lessons or went to dance school. I was terrified to dance in the open what I was teaching the children in the beginning. My friend, my pastor's wife Carmen would come and sit in the back pew of the church watching me teach and dance with the children. She'd encouraged me to dance after I taught her after school program children to dance and mime. Finally I did. The first time I was shaking all over. But then something happened inside me. A fire was lit to worship and all I could see when I moved was God. It didn't matter who else was around. It helped when I kept my eyes closed too. People were distracting. From the very beginning, Gerry supported me with music. He helped me record music, some of which I was able to record my own voice with an intro when he played it. He would also videotape the ministry. He made sure I had the best equipment there was for what I was doing before I knew I needed it. There were times he and I ministered together with him playing the saxophone and I danced. He could play music by ear, but also took lessons later. We as a family, our girls and us ministered together as well.

We were united in the things we did even though we liked different things. Just like he was my partner in worship. Prior to my ministry in movement, he was president of the little league, and I partnered him by operating the concession stand. He needed someone he could trust with the cash flow in order to get the league back into the black from the previous president. With the older kids, our KP's, (kids prior to our marriage) now adults and gone; we spent more time with our girls. They were at our hip with everything. They played little league and learned how to count money too watching how I worked the concessions. We had our first family vacation ever taking the auto train to Florida for Gerry's family reunion of sorts. It was small, just a handful of people on his mothers side.

We loved the train trip together. It was an adventure for all of us. We went to Universal Studios then drove up to Atlanta touring the sites on our way back home. Thankfully one of Gerry's friends met us in the Carolina's and drove the rest of the way home. We kept the girls active, staying involved with all they did. They were both dance majors while attending the original Camden Creative Arts High School. They danced on the dance team with the Camden High School Marching Band that went to President Obama's inauguration. Gerry and I sat proudly watching television knowing our girls were in Washington enjoying this once in a lifetime historic event.

The four of us were together at one of the campaign headquarters the night Barack won the election. Driving out of the event home, we stopped to collect a huge Obama/Biden sign on the way home. It was Gerry's idea of course; he was crazy like that. He's the bold one and I'm scared by the book Betty, afraid of getting caught. There was another level of Gerry when we cruised together. Well, not just him. I cut loose too. I have videos of some of them to remember. Gerry was pulled up on stage for shows, I won karaoke. Something we'd probably never do around people who knew us. We even won the perfect couple award on our final cruise being outrageous. For the most part we both tend to be reserved, respectable, dignified in public but when we don't know anybody and can cut loose, who cares. I think it had something to do with both our upbringing and appearances in public. We can be as crazy as it gets and laugh about it. That was at least our thought. He brought that out of me when I was with him. We were silly romantic too, him giving me a lap dance on a couples retreat to Bruno Mars "That's what I like". I still smile thinking of him whenever I hear that song. The best place to be for me was wrapped in his arms. It's the only place I wanted to be at the end of the day. No matter what, we always know we will be together in bed at the end of the evening. That's all that mattered. Gerry always said he had trouble sleeping if I was not beside him. We were meant to share our bed.

We had our rough times too like every couple. A real marriage has its trials. There were times we hurt one another deeply. I dare you to find a couple together over twenty five years who did not hurt one anothers feelings at some time. In all our years of marriage we never once seriously considered ending what we had. Renewing our vows and dedication at 23 years proved that even with Egypt and her kids choosing to not come. Though disappointing for Gerry, there was far too much good than bad in us together. Like two candles melted together, the wax intertwined. We could not be separated into two individual candles as before. And there were people who secretly or so they thought, who tried coming between us. A few really think they had, ending up disappointed in the end. Out of sight was never out of mind. We could be miles apart yet still very much together. If he was hurt or needed me I'd move mountains to get to him and he'd do the same for me. It didn't matter if we had a major fight an hour before. What we had was just that deep, planted by God.

We always belonged to the same church since he gave his life to Christ, with the same pastor who counseled us before marriage, married us, baptized us, christened our children and came to our bedside in the hospital. Rev. Calvin R. Woods, he is truly one in a trillion. When he was retired and the new pastor coming in had a different direction, the Lord showed me it was time for me to leave. He actually directed me to leave three years earlier but I was talked into staying. The delay was not a good thing. This time it was clear. It was a difficult decision as well. I had grown much under Pastor Woods. It also meant not being with my husband in the same church for the first time, along with not really being sure where to go. It felt like being in the wilderness for a while, even joining a local church to be close, until my friend Tamika told me about The Perfecting Church. We now belonged to two different churches at this time. Gerry remained to serve over the food ministry at the Parkside Camden church after a good friend passed away. He promised his friend Ken Russell another man of God full of compassion for people, he would keep the food program going. As a man of integrity, Gerry kept his word. The church had changed and he wasn't happy there, he stayed to serve the people in the community. He'd come to church with me once a month. I wanted him to be with me where he would continue to be fed spiritually. He liked TPC and the way Pastor Kevin delivered the message. I just had to understand his commitment to his word and the needs of the many outweigh my needs for the time.

As a minister of movement who birthed the dance ministry at Parkside UMC, I was asked to minister in dance for

Love

watchnight, New Years Eve 2019. At first Gerry didn't want me to. He was dead set against it due to his personal feelings I fully understood. There have been a lot of changes and divisions going on in the Camden church. Our girls had stopped attending. One refused to return. I was no longer there and he was there only to serve those outside the church who came for food. He didn't want me in the midst of that and didn't understand why I would minister there. I told him as I prayed on it as I do with any request to minister in movement; there was a message to be given at that time. God wanted me there. He understood after I explained, as he usually did. He hadn't seen me minister very much since I left the church and my ministry. On this night, we were back together like we used to be. I had no worries with him there in the media booth. He played my music like he always did in the past. Mine was the final message in movement prior to the pastor welcoming the new year. It was a combination of two Tasha Cobbs songs; Gracefully Broken and He Knows My Name. I brought God's word finishing just before midnight. I didn't know the message was as much for me, as it was for the church. At midnight, Gerry met me at the altar. I could see the tears in his eyes. His words "I love to see you dance" filled my heart with words I hadn't heard in some time. Words I cherished as much as I cherished him. We embraced and kissed, washing away the issues of the present year looking forward to a bright year ahead where we'd celebrate 30 years of marriage and his retirement. Our children were now all adults and we could finally just enjoy one another. 2020 would finally be our time.

Loss

"If my people, who are called by my name, shall humble themselves, and pray, and seek my face, and turn from their wicked ways; then will I here from heaven, and will forgive their sin, and will heal their land".
2 Chronicles 7:14

We closed our eyes on December 31, 2019 with hope of the new year. We awoke to the world we were once used to never being the same. We were not expecting to wake up to a nightmare to follow in a matter of weeks. Though this is my loss during the Covid pandemic as tragic as it is for me. It does not lessen the impact of all the other losses that took place during the pandemic, especially in this way.

As we entered 2020 it seemed everyone was getting sick from cold or flu virus. I was sick for a straight week like never before. I called out from serving at my church afraid of getting anyone sick. Gerry was faithful by my side, taking care of me and our daughter who was also sick. Gerry was well. There were rumors of a sickness coming from China.

January 21 — CDC Confirms First US Coronavirus Case

A Washington state resident becomes the first person in the United States with a confirmed case of the 2019 novel coronavirus, having returned from Wuhan on January 15, thanks to overnight polymerase chain reaction testing.

By February, the world learned this virus infected cruise ships, the first on February 4, the Diamond Princess quarantined in Japan. The World Health Organization declared the COVID-19 outbreak a pandemic on March 11, 2020. We had no idea how our world would forever be changed. I had no idea how quickly my world would change. By now daily news reports were overrun by reports of people getting COVID and the death count began rising. There was no known cure at the time. We were told to wear masks, spray disinfectant, wear gloves and use hand sanitizer. Supplies were limited to purchase in stores as people began to stockpile in panic causing supplies to run out quickly. Companies were calling on sewers to make masks for employees. My friend Sherry called from Campbell Soup asking if I would make 100 masks. I began sewing right away. Gerry was my model for a man's size. I made masks for my family as well though supplies were so scarce. Egypt came by the house bringing us some masks from the hospital where she worked when it began. Gerry watched the news steadily. I could not watch it anymore.

I did everything I could think of to avoid getting sick. I boiled citrus peels on the stove with salt inhaling the

Loss

steam being told this would kill the virus before it gets in. We of course wore all the protective gear possible when we left our house which had become rare. I was now cooking meals for my in-laws. This was because Mister no longer wanted to eat Sweety's cooking. Her dementia was increasing to where she was becoming forgetful. She either was not cooking or not cooking like she used to. With him being a diabetic I wanted to make sure Mister didn't eat too much of the wrong thing and that Sweety continued to eat.

Sweety liked my cooking, she could relax and enjoy it. I cooked their meals vacuum sealing them so all they had to do was warm it up. Gerry and I, masked up, would take a box I'd fill with food to their home, handing it to them on the outside porch. We did not go inside considering the conditions, wanting to keep everyone as safe as possible. They appreciated the box, especially Sweety. I usually made them homemade soup, a favorite for Mister. I spoke with Sweety every day just to make sure she was ok. By this time, she was calling at least three times a day back-to-back not realizing I just spoke with her. A sign the dementia was growing. I felt sad for her, she had been such a vibrant woman.

March 16, 2020, our New Jersey Gov. Phil Murphy announced statewide restrictions beginning at 8pm. That was the curfew for everyone to be home. Business operations were limited and schools were closed. For those still in operation people had to be six feet apart. Everywhere you went in markets, hospitals or office buildings there were markings on the floors to stand six feet apart, and wear masks. Most offices limited the number of people in an area on the floor to comply with our governor's mandate. It was all in order to save as many lives as possible. The bad news was non-stop as the death numbers rose. We heard stories of people taking their loved ones to the hospital, only to have them taken away and never seen again. It was terrifying. Most were put on respirators where they ultimately died of the disease. What was worse is with so many deaths happening so quickly, some bodies could not be buried for weeks. In some major cities, people were placed in refrigerated storage containers waiting for burial. It was a horrible thought, my heart ached for those families. I just couldn't watch the reports anymore, I didn't want to hear it. I surely didn't want to live it.

Gerry and I were thankful for the curfew. I could see him and he could see me, we were safe together. All the crap we went through the year prior was erased, meaningless. What was really important was, we were together. Prior to this horrific pandemic, we were so busy living and doing for others, we lost time with one another. 8pm became a magic hour for us. We started getting excited as the hour arrived and we could be shut in together. We began spending time talking again like we used to while I sewed masks. He said people at his job wanted my masks but of course didn't want to pay for them. I gave the mask to most people, friends, whether they paid me

Loss

or not. It was more about saving lives than money. I was scared but felt comfortable with all the precautions my hero was taking to protect our home and all of us in it. He was like the white lion; strong, rare but gentle king of the jungle. He is our protector. He is my king. It seemed that the statewide curfew and isolation would be for a while. Gerry purchased a chess set so he could finally teach me how to play chess. It's a beautiful set made of wood.

Our oldest daughter Deborah, as a first responder, had to go out every day. She generally worked late nights or overnight. We kept the micro band disinfectant at the door where she sprayed her clothes and herself off as she entered. Gerry generally was up to listen for her to get in. That was their special time to talk. She worked most nights. We didn't see our youngest daughter as much. She no longer lived at home but would check in to see how we were or if we needed anything. We kept in contact by phone. I wished and wanted her to move back home but wasn't at the place to convince her and Gerry wasn't going to do it. He wanted her to make her own decision and move at her own pace. So, in my frustration I just prayed for the best.

It was an unexpected surprise when she came to us telling us she was pregnant. My response was not the best mixed with so many emotions about her life at that moment and now having a baby during a pandemic. My fear and anxiety meter went off the chart and came out of my mouth the wrong way. Gerry scolded and corrected me, making me see the blessing in even this. I got myself in check and was able to embrace her with the love and encouragement she deserved.

As we came into the month of April many people began working from home. Our governor gave a list of essential workers. These were people we could not do without. These were people on the front line who in most cases, could not do their jobs from home. They consisted of medical staff, police officers, fire fighters, financial institutions and some county workers which included my husband. Even city hall was shut down.

Our younger daughter, Tinisha, who works in the banking industry gave her job notice that she would not come back into the building after finding out someone tested positive for Covid. She had not only herself to think of, but the baby she was carrying. Her job made accommodations for her to work from home with a computer by the grace of God. They were able to accommodate most of their employees to work at home for safety and continue the work needed. For that they are to be applauded. They cared about their business, but they cared about their employees too.

It grew more difficult to get through to any government offices as buildings closed and adjustments were made for home workers. Their phone lines became overwhelmed with people trying to get through to put in papers for retirement and other issues. Gerry was one of those people

Loss

trying to finalize papers for his retirement in June. Just in time for our thirtieth wedding anniversary.

Gerry, who I considered fearless, usually took the train to work but felt unsafe on public transportation with the more the death toll and spread of this virus climbed. I asked him if he could work from home like everyone else seemed to be doing. I actually was begging for him to be home during this scary time. He told me it was not possible with his position. He told me he had to go into his work building to do his job making sure families continued to receive their food and medical benefits. Though he was considered an essential worker, his work had to be done on the agency computer in the agency building. I just didn't understand why he had to be the one going in when he was about to retire. He worked there for thirty-five years. Again I asked why it had to be him. He told me if he did not go in with cases backing up, people would not get their food and health benefits. There were already a lot of people who had bailed out taking stress and other leaves during that time. It was essential for him to be there in that building doing the work. He considered the needs of others over his own, going into a building that was old, built in 1955 the same year Gerry was born with no windows and historically unhealthy.

The conditions were not good. The building was originally built and served as a showcase department store. It was bricked over with no windows and converted into an office building where he worked those thirty-five years.

It had a history of health issues which included rodents and asbestos, expected in a building this old. They were in the process of trying to move and tear the building down. Now with the pandemic the building was neither cleaned nor in compliance with the governors directive. Workers, those who remained were in close proximity to one another. They were given one mask to keep for protection, and many people didn't wear it while coughing, spreading germs. Gerry wore the masks I made him and would switch as needed. He purchased his own hand sanitizer, gloves and spray disinfectant too trying to protect himself in unsafe conditions because the job did not supply it. Gerry tried his best to keep his personal space shielded in unsafe conditions. That's a difficult thing to do when you are sitting in the middle of the fire.

He did this while trying to reassure me he would not be working in those conditions much longer. He will be retiring in June. In June we would be free to have uninterrupted time for vacations and whatever else we wanted to do. He would no longer be going into that building to work. But right now, there was no choice. I didn't like it and was scared. His voice of calm gave a little hope, but not much given the situation. Because he felt unsafe taking public transportation, I began driving Gerry to and from work. That's the least I could do and best I could do to protect him in getting there and coming home again. Prayer had to cover what went on inside.

Loss

Tinisha came by the house April 21 very excited with news she wanted to share with us. It was her first ultrasound showing she was 10 weeks pregnant. I was in the living room when she handed me an ultrasound picture. Immediately I saw it. TWINS!!!! OMG!!! Being a twin myself I always wanted twins, but our daughter is having them instead. I couldn't be happier. We ran upstairs to where Gerry was to share the good news. He was standing in the bathroom getting ready for his day. She handed the photo to him saying "look daddy"! Gerry took the photo in his hands and looked at it squinting his eyes. He asked what it was. With excitement, we repeated "look!" Though he knew it was the ultrasound, he said he didn't have his contacts in to see what we wanted. Finally, I told him "the ultrasound, there are two, twins". He smiled and said "REALLY"! "Isn't that something". We then let him finish getting ready. We didn't know then, that was the last time our youngest daughter would see her dad alive.

Another week of world horror continued but Gerry and I were excited to finally become the grandparents we always wanted to be. Gerry had other grandchildren and great grandchildren through Egypt and Israel but they did not allow him to be an active part of their lives on a regular basis because of their feelings toward me. At least Egypt didn't. She lived locally making it possible for Gerry to spend regular time with them. But she didn't. Israel didn't have as much active access with his children through three marriages nor made the effort to make it happen. It hurt Gerry but he would never show it. He most definitely would not tell them. He just tried to make the most of those moments he got to see them. He made sure to include them on the list for Christmas gifts for the food program he led. His one request was for the children to come get them, the one time he knew he'd see them. The parents made sure they picked up the gifts even when the kids weren't with them. Tinisha's pregnancy brought great joy to us. We knew this would be different. Gerry would finally get to be the grandfather he was meant to be spending time with our new babies. God was finally answering my prayer to be a grandparent and He's doing it by sending two, one for each of us. Words could not express our excitement, at least not mine. I waited a long time for this. Each day I'd tell Gerry we're going to be grandparents of twins. If only that was the way things turned out.

We continued steadfast with our personal precautions. Gerry always had sinus problems. They would act up when it got cold. This winter was bitter cold. His sinus issues were getting worse. He was on medication he really didn't like and called the doctor about it. His doctor instructed him to continue with the medication. At this time during the pandemic conditions had gotten so bad you could not go directly to the hospital if you thought you had Covid. That is unless you could not breath. You had to contact your doctor for an appointment first and see if they felt your condition was a concern. Even then appointments were not in person, you saw them through video on a screen.

We began living in a virtual society. We saw our doctor on a computer or phone screen. Meetings, bible studies, churches were done through Zoom, Facebook, YouTube and other social media sites. Gerry's sinuses got no better. Then he began feeling unwell. I don't know when it began, he would often hide some things from me. It was a two fold thing, him not wanting me to worry so much if he considered it a part of his normal life. He felt there was no need for me to worry. Like his vision. Or if it were something more serious that needed care and I found out, I'd go into action without thought. I'd do anything to take care of him even if he didn't want it. My vow was to protect and look after him no matter what.

On the afternoon of April 27, Gerry told me he made an appointment with his doctor for the next morning. I was concerned but not frantic. I had asked him just a day or so earlier when he seemed sluggish, if he was alright. He told me it was his sinuses. I thought that was what the appointment was for. That night as we were going to bed he told me to sleep downstairs on the sofa because if he was sick with Covid, he didn't want me to get it. He also asked for a big glass of ice with cold water. In hindsight, I wish I didn't give him cold water. But I did as he asked, still believing God everything was ok.

We did everything we were supposed to. With faith I trust God not expecting Covid to come to our door. However, about 2am on April 28th our daughter Deborah who happened to not be working this night came and woke me up. She said "Mom, we have to get dad to the hospital now". I jumped up from the sofa and ran upstairs to our bedroom. I saw Gerry struggling with putting on clothes. Deborah said he would not let her help him. I began helping him get dressed. I don't know what I had on. As long as I was covered, I didn't care. We made it down the stairs and got him in the car. As fast as I could I went through every light regardless of color racing him to the hospital as I prayed begging and pleading for him NOT to have Covid. I could take anything else but Covid. He could recover from anything else as long as it wasn't COVID. GOD PLEASE DON'T DO THIS TO ME!!!!

We pulled into the emergency room at the hospital. Deborah ran in first to alert them. A wheelchair was brought out for Gerry. By the time I could close the door and follow into the hospital they already had him behind the exam room. I was locked out, not allowed back there with him. All I could do was wait giving information at the desk. The entire time I'm praying please don't let it be covid. I'm first told his oxygen rate was at 70% which is not good. Next, I'm told he has pneumonia. Still hopeful, I'm begging God please let it just be the pneumonia, let him get better. He can recover from pneumonia. Then I get the dreaded report, words no one wants to hear "he is positive for COVID-19". That's the moment time stood still. I don't know if I heard the nurses next words. I was in a tunnel, everything went dark and my ears were clogged. When I became aware again, she said she had

Loss

to get him on oxygen. They wouldn't let me see him and I had no contact with him.

Every nightmare I avoided watching and hearing on the television for months was now happening to me and my family. I couldn't breathe. "NOOOOO, NOT GERRY!!!! I contacted our kids telling them to pray that he was in the hospital. This was prior to receiving the Covid results. At the time our youngest didn't know how bad it was, no one did. She thought he would be ok. I was glad she didn't know at the time with her being pregnant. I'm thankful, her last moment with her dad was a happy one. I had no way to contact Gerry. I was in a panic not knowing what to do. I felt helpless and alone. Gerry was my hero, the white lion of protection over us. He had his phone but it could not be found at first. I drove all the way home looking for it in case he left it there. It was not. Deborah let me know the hospital staff finally located his phone among his things.

I sent him a text, April 28, 2020 6:16am

"Praying down heaven on you. When I video call don't speak. I just want to see your face. You are strong, FIGHT."

When he got it, he facetimed me. This is the only time we ever did this. Maybe one time before. We had no need to. He tried to remain brave and calm for me as he struggled to breath with the oxygen on. I was breaking inside trying to hold on for him. He knew me well. I knew him too. His oxygen level was dropping, so the hospital wanted to put him on a respirator quickly. We only had a brief time to speak. The hospital was trying to rush to get him on the equipment. As we facetimed, I asked Gerry if going on the respirator was what he wanted. He told me "yes". His eyes smiled for me. Yet I know there was fear too for both of us. I survived being on a respirator before, but we saw the news reports. We heard about the others who came down this road. It is horrifying. I tried my best to push past fear to faith, hoping he'd overcome this.

While speaking, Egypt called. He told me, let me talk to her and he'd call me back. In no more than thirty seconds he called me right back knowing the hospital was pressing. We knew I would not be able to see him and I would be unable to talk to him either after this moment. I hung on to him as long as I could. Again, I asked if he was sure about the respirator. He repeated "yes". He then told me "I love you; I'll see you in a few days'" . I told him I loved him too. Those are the final words I heard from my beloved. Those are the last words he ever heard. Those are the final words he spoke while here on earth. Those are the final words that keep my heart beating here to complete the work we began together. I will always love him. He closed his eyes knowing he was purely loved.

Deborah and I returned home without Gerry, speechless. All we could do is cry together. Had it not been for Deborah, Gerry would have died in our bedroom with me on the sofa. That may have been his plan. I don't know if I could have lived with that. I believe he knew he had Covid but didn't want me to know so he could die at home where he found his peace. Not die in a hospital away from family. But God's grace in Deborah being off duty that night and a night owl allowed her to hear his struggle alerting me. I only wish she too got to say goodbye and hear his "I love you" to her. It was there. I know he meant it, had he seen her on the phone he would have given it. Time just moves so quickly when in that position. The trauma of this night for her was too great along with those that followed where she stepped in her father's shoes being my strength. Deborah was the one keeping me from completely falling apart. She took on weight she should not have had to while she too was overwhelmed.

After getting home, I contacted Gerry's parents and siblings, calling each of them to tell them what had happened, asking them to pray. Only prayer would bring him through this by God's will. Those I reached understood except for one. His younger brother, Dale. When I called telling him about Gerry, asking for him and his wife Rosa to pray, his response was. "Man, I know I haven't been there much for my brother but now he's going to....." I stopped him by saying "DON'T SAY IT!" He continued anyway with the word "die". Everything in me went cold. At that point there was nothing more I wanted to hear from or say to them. Politeness allowed me to continue holding onto the phone, though my ears stopped listening. All I wanted to do was hang up, and hang up fast. His words spoke death over my husband. There was no coming back from that for me given what I am currently facing. It was like he didn't care at all after all the times Gerry had been there for him. He didn't give a thought what Gerry's family was going through even if he didn't give two hoots about me personally. If one can be so careless with words coming out of your mouth at such a tender time, who knows what will come from their mouth the next. I had never heard him say or do anything complimentary nor connected to faith in any way towards another in 30 years, so I blame myself for expecting anything different. My primary purpose and obligation was to let his family know his condition. That I did.

April 28, 2020 to May 2, 2020 were the longest days of my life. I couldn't eat, I barely slept. To be real, I don't know how often I took a shower for fear of missing a call from the hospital. Sweety continues to call repeatedly, I'm not sure if she realizes Gerry's condition. I went to my PCell asking them to lift Gerry up in prayer. Any and everybody I knew who had a relationship with Christ whether I knew them on a personal level or not, I asked to pray in faith for his recovery. I had no pride. This was not about pride, it was about healing. I did not move from my sofa day and night.

I contacted his job letting them know the situation of all that happened. They sent me worker's compensation papers to fill out for Gerry's work-related illness. I've never had to fill out this type of paperwork not realizing

Loss

he would be covered. I wasn't even thinking about that though it was a blessing. I just wanted Gerry back home. I lay in a permanent spot on the sofa day and night by the phone for the daily calls from the hospital just to hear he is still alive. If he is alive there is hope. I trusted and believed in God's promises that he would not take Gerry from me. All I could think of was Gerry. I packed up my sewing machine and the masks I was making, putting it all away. None of it mattered to me anymore. The one person I wanted to protect was out of my reach.

I got calls from different people praying for him and for me. One sister in Christ, Andrea prayed with me one day. I felt the power of heaven come down so strong as I laid stretched out on my living room floor washed in tears. I believe and even saw Gerry walk out the front doors of that hospital healthy, strong and whole again. Without a doubt in my mind, I saw it. The sun was bright as he came out the doors. For that moment I was able to exhale with hope. Every day I waited to hear the doctors report, anything positive along with the vision from this prayer kept me hanging on. This prayer kept that hope alive that everything would be alright like it was when I was sick on a respirator for months. I eventually came back home.

Hope didn't last long. When Gerry first went in, doctors saw him as a strong healthy person. They wanted to do a procedure called ECMO, a procedure that is a form of life support for people with life-threatening illness or injury that affects the function of their heart or lungs. ECMO keeps blood moving through the body and keeps blood gasses (oxygen and carbon dioxide) in balance. However, they could not do this for Gerry due to him having pulmonary hypertension. Gerry had surgery years earlier to have a thymoma removed from his chest. They had to cut one of the nerves to his diaphragm. It severely limited his breathing on one side. His condition where breathing was concerned at this point was similar to mine. His condition affected the side of the chest where the ECMO would go so they could not do it. They gave him blood with antibodies and were hopeful waiting on new medication to come from New York. We just had to wait a few more days.

The time between the doctor's report for ECMO and waiting for the medication for Gerry was not good. Each day, he was alive I thank God, but some of him was deteriorating. His white and red blood cells were out of whack and his oxygen level was not good. He began losing pulse in his extremities. I tried to believe with hope holding the image from that prayer of Gerry walking out of the hospital but I know what the medical reports meant. I spent enough time in the hospital myself to know.

Then came early morning May 3, 2020. I felt something was not right. I tried to push it aside as fear creeped up my back. The phone rang in the middle of the night. I saw the hospital number come up on the caller ID. When I picked it up no one was there. I called the hospital right back but was unable to get the nurse who took care of Gerry like I normally could. I was told they would contact me. I was nervous trying not to think it was bad. I called the hospital again in the morning closer to the time I generally spoke with someone. I was told again the nurse was not available and they would contact me. Again, I pushed myself to have hope this Sunday morning as I prepared for church service.

Like I said, we were living in a virtual society. Church services were virtual since the pandemic. I watched the church service as normal. It was good. Shortly after service ended that changed. I received a call from the hospital. The doctor told me Gerry's heart had stopped. They were going to work on him to see if it comes back but then will discontinue so he would not have brain damage. My heart stopped beating too. This could not be happening. The hospital was expecting a new medication to come from New York the next day. I just needed him to hold on for the miracle. His heart had to restart. He had to be alright. They put a phone to his ear so I could talk to him as he left this life for his forever home. I didn't know what to say except to tell him how much I love him and didn't want him to go, I want him to stay and fight. That was not fair. I should have told him to go in peace. I should have told him how much I loved him and how he filled my life with joy. I should have told him he was the perfect man and perfect husband for me. I should have told him how happy I was to have his children and what a good father he was and now he can rest knowing one day we would be together again. May 3, 2020, Gerry did walk out those hospital doors on that bright day. I just didn't see the glow of the wings he wore before he took flight. Deborah remained by my side for every call and every tear, with me not realizing she was crying on her own alone. All we had was each other.

I called Tinisha and the other kids were notified. Tinisha contacted Mister who seemed more interested in who was driving him to his eye appointment that week. He showed little response over hearing the son he relied on and who was at his beck and call has died. Tinisha was going to take him to his eye appointment for me since I was concerned about my Covid status not yet revealed since taking Gerry to the hospital. I was supposed to be in isolation. She came to the house in spite of everything to make sure we were alright. When Tinisha told me of Mister's response, seeing the pain in her eyes, I told her I'd take him. Tinisha met my friend Arlene at the door with flowers to bring me when she came. Arlene did not know Gerry had just died. She was taken off guard and upset as she left for our loss.

A flood of calls began after that. I tried to respond to most of them, but it became too much for me. Deborah began to take calls and we asked people to give me some time. I was overwhelmed by the love and care of so many for Gerry. People sent us food I could not eat, cards with money, flowers, plants. All these things meant more than anyone can imagine in a time of no physical touch. I had no girlfriend who could come to embrace me or comfort us. There was no one to help directly in what I needed to do. I didn't know what to do. This is the first death I had to prepare for. It was easy for me to handle things while Gerry was here to take the lead. But now he's gone. Neither of my pastors, my past or current could come see about me. Pastor Woods would have been here. He has been here for everything vital in Gerry and my life since marrying us. This is a man who drove 500 miles to North Carolina to my hospital bedside to pray for me, then turned around and drove right back to New Jersey. Only a pandemic could hold him back. For his safety I wouldn't want him to come. As much as I was grateful for the overwhelming love and support from people, I was mad at God. I don't think I have ever been angrier with God than the day He allowed Gerry to die. How and why would he bring Gerry into my life with all the love I had for him only to have him leave in this way. I told Him "You don't make promises, You give options!" However, I had enough fear and respect for God not to say much more. He knew the depth of my hurt and pain. I am His daughter. He also knew I would get through it better than I did at that moment. My world came crashing into pieces and there was nothing I could do about it. I just sat in a daze reading the scripture I had on my wall. "If ye ABIDE in me, and my WORDS abide in you, ask whatsoever ye will, and it shall be done unto YOU". John 15:7 I didn't see how that could be true. God's word was in me with strong faith. Why didn't He give me Gerry's life back? Only God knew the answer.

Gerry and I served at far too many funerals at our former church to the extent I knew it was not what I wanted. I did not want to ignite the pain of my loss all over again to show others nor leave my family with the expense it brought. I told Gerry how I felt and he quietly listened with understanding. Big funerals were not what he looked forward to dealing with. He said he didn't know how he would handle things if and when his parents died with them growing in age. In their mid eighties now. Gerry and I only briefly discussed our burial wishes. I expected to be gone before him seeking out how and where I wanted to be buried. Gerry only stated what he did not want or where he did not want to be buried. He did not want to be buried in Camden where he spent his whole life. He was adamant about not being buried up the street from our home. Anything other than that appeared to be alright with him. We chose a natural burial to go directly back to the earth God created. There would be no filling the body with poison or embalming fluid to preserve a body that is already dead, no expensive casket placed in a vault in the ground delaying the natural process of life. There is nothing wrong with those who choose this way or cremation if that is one's choice. I just wanted my burial to be simple and quick so those I love can go back to their lives without extending their grieving. The time I spend here on earth with them and how I live my life during that time is what's important. So, now I had to do something I never planned or had to do before. I only had hope what I chose for me is what Gerry wanted for himself, and we would be together.

Loss

I contacted the funeral home associated with the burial place to pick up Gerry's remains. Since he has not been preserved, his body much like the Jewish or Muslim custom has to be buried quickly before decay. He died on Sunday; the burial would take place on Wednesday. In this pandemic, I was thankful my husband could be buried right away and not sit in a container waiting somewhere. What was difficult was the number of people you could have at a burial, even outside. I was limited to having ten people at his burial and possibly one or two more. Immediately I counted along with myself our collective five children, his parents and three brothers. I went to bed that night planning on calling and letting them know the next day. However, when I got up in prayer the Lord said "No". I questioned it wondering why.

I began to think about Gerry, reflecting on the few things he did say. His love and fear of losing his parents, realizing it was all on him. His brothers never helped when he asked. Mister had been sick fighting a bad cold. We were getting mediation he could take as a diabetic especially since he faced a few close calls where we had to call an ambulance. He also had to use the bathroom quite often. Sweety was not steady on her feet walking since she had broken her hip a year earlier. I watched how she walked, often dragging her feet and could easily trip on the vines that protrude out of the ground. She had mood swings and short term memory loss with her dementia. With both of them not in good health conditions and me not knowing my own covid status it would not be safe for them to be there. Getting them there was another issue because I could not drive them in my car. It was an hour away, the weather cold and damp that day.

Then there were his brothers. The question was, "who are his brothers?" Gerry had three brothers he could not depend on. Over time it weighed on and bothered him without him saying much. He made every effort to be the best support to them as possible. Roman and Samual lived in the area. He made sure they had food every time they called. We packed it up and delivered it to them at their door. They never came to pick it up, nor would they go to the food program to pick it up. He gave them money too on the sly thinking I didn't know. It was a man thing. When Dale showed up from New York the rare times he did, Gerry got him Eagle gear since he was a fan and of course he also paid the bill if they went out. Gerry was smarter than all of them, even if they were physically capable of doing things he couldn't. He listened to them, counseled them and picked up the slack when it came to their parents. But it was reaching a point of wearing on Gerry when he was the only one giving. It showed when he stopped me from planning gatherings to include his entire family. No more Thanksgiving dinners, cook outs and Christmas making sure all the kids got something. He began to focus on our family alone. His oldest brother Samuel accompanied Gerry on the train ride to Raleigh when I was sick to keep him company. He resembled Hulk Hogan back then to a kid on the train. It was at Gerry's expense of course. Samuel did give Gerry an occasional birthday card. In the thirty years; I recall seeing two. His next brother, Roman, stayed pretty much to himself. If Gerry needed some work done Roman could do, he'd call him. He didn't pay him much because, as Gerry would say, he was always giving Roman stuff. And of course, there was the youngest, Dale. When he and Rosa weren't at odds, they'd come down from New York like they were special guests to eat and drink. Sweety used to be close to Rosa when they married a year before us. Rosa was always buying Sweety jewelry as if to buy her love. She had a little money back then. But over the years Sweety began to think less and less of Rosa due to multiple issues to the point she didn't want to see her at all. But because she was Dale's wife she tolerated her the same way Rosa tolerated me at her convenience. Sweety was sweet to everyone, but was always glad to see her leave.

Rosa brought the grandchildren and great grands most times when she came around which meant a lot. Usually without Dale. Listening to Rosa, their relationship was shaky up, down, on and off. She mostly spoke in the negative about him to me about how she didn't want him around. At one time she didn't want her daughter around either. She only wanted her grandchildren. It benefited her to stay with him, so they remained married.

Of the three, Roman was my favorite if I had to pick one. He seemed to have the most compassionate heart most closely like Gerry's. He faced hard times with his family, primarily Mister could not, nor would forgive keeping him in the safe place at a distance. If he needed something I never minded taking it to him. I would check on him if he was in the hospital and bring him something to eat. Nevertheless, the situation was what Gerry wanted. Who did he want to stand as his brother? It was not about me, nor was it about any of them, their feelings or blood.

The final decision came from the last thing Gerry said to me regarding his brothers if anything were to happen to their parents. I won't repeat it in this writing, but it's the first time I felt and saw Gerry's total sign off when it came to his brothers. I believe seeing his parents in the state they were in at the time, the house, their health and so much more with four capable adult sons and him being the only one taking care of them, was too much. It reached a limit. It was also so unfair. Two brothers lived just minutes away. Samuel was there often but didn't take on the role we did. Roman to me seemed to feel he wasn't wanted by Mister. That was unless it was a planned event, by Mister which included a family photo op. Dale just refused to come to Camden. Gerry loved his brothers, but didn't like them much. He made that clear.

Then there were three guys that were important to Gerry. Many of Gerry's close friends had passed weighing on him greatly the last few years. He still had a few close friends. Some I could not reach at the time. But then there were these three he depended on who were closer than any brother. These three have been there for him through the years. They celebrated with him, worked with him, had fun with him and served with him. There is not a week that went by when Gerry did not talk with these guys, his brothers; Phil, George and Kevin. I contacted them to be there for Gerry one last time. I knew I would be at great odds with Mister and the boys but my responsibility to the end was to my husband, not them. They in turn made their feelings known, standing behind the actions of Mister. They had no concern for Gerry, or our family even after all the times we stood behind them. They were never there for Gerry when he lived but now angry to not stand over him now that he is gone. It was now about getting back at me or getting even with me, the outsider for not doing things Mister's way. But considering how Mister was, the events that follow may have occurred anyway, even if they were at the burial.

Who Am I

Who am I but the dust of the earth
Tiny grains of sand molded together like a sand castle on the beach
Each grain representing a stage, moment, event in my life
The highs, lows, laughter and yes, tears which bind those grains together to give them form
Yes, I am grains of sand molded together by His love
His life breathed into me to perfection placed in a world of disaster doing everything it can to block my light
Wind, rain, snow, heat, trauma, disease all elements to tear down my physical
Lies, rumors, threats, abuse to breakdown my mind causing doubt of self-worth
Yet, I rise from within by the strength and power poured down deep into the mold of my heart He created
His blood warm healing every wound allowing me to break forth rising from the ashes meant for me
Not today, I'm free
That's who I am
Selah

Baleeia Minggia (2021)

Abandoned

Even if my father and mother abandon me, the LORD will hold me close. Psalm 27:10 (NLT)

I don't believe there are any bad people in the world. The bible tells us God created everything and that everything that He created was good. God created us, and since everything He created is good, we cannot be bad. However, God also gave us freedom of choice in the decisions we make with accountability. Therefore, everyone has the choice to do what is right, wrong, good or bad. The path one takes is their own. If we journey in the wrong direction God stands with His arms outstretched giving us the ability to repent and do what is right. Some do, others don't. There is no personal judgment against those written about in this chapter. I am simply sharing the truth and facts of the matter. The names have been changed for the sake of not wanting to have their actual names on record. They know who they are and those who know us. I ask you not to allow the facts of what occurred form a negative opinion of them as they have done nothing to affect your life. Nor an opinion of me, I am stating my truth and facts of what occurred. Just understand, and learn as I have, if anything in your life parallels. Find a way to forgive.

It was Monday, one day after Gerry died. I didn't know how I was going to make it from day to day without him.

I am on permanent social security disability from lung damage, have a mortgage, car payment, monthly bills well beyond what I can afford alone. I paid the bills, but he was the breadwinner and provider. His income is what made our life work. Beyond taking care of the mortgage which I did, I had no idea how I was going to live. And the girls were now leaning on me. I needed Gerry much more than for the financial stability he provided. He knew how to handle every situation that now I had to figure out with just the memory of his words in my ear to guide me.It's not that I couldn't do things, I was independent when he met me. When I became his wife, I let go of control, submitting it to him. Now I have to plan and come up with funds to say goodbye.

I needed to have five thousand dollars for the cemetery to put his remains in the ground prior to his burial. We had been waiting on the stimulus checks the governor was releasing since the pandemic. That would have helped greatly. I did not have that amount of money in our accounts and Gerry had not gotten paid. Mister was pretty well off financially and was more than capable of providing for his son. I have never asked him for anything, especially not money. It has always been difficult for me to ask for help in general from anyone. Even with Gerry it was hard for me to tell him at times when I needed something. I was raised to handle things on my own. That is what I learned to do. This time I needed help. The help wasn't for me, it was for Gerry. I will always ask for help for my family before I ask for help for myself. I talked to my good friend Tamika telling her my dilemma and my apprehension in making this call to his father. I was thankful I had a friend I could be so open with who had compassion and understanding. She told me if I needed her help to let her know.

I took a deep breath and made the call. I told him the situation, that I needed five thousand dollars for Gerry to put in the ground asking if he would help. He first asked, "doesn't Gerry have life insurance?" I told him he did and that I was trying to locate it. I just would not have it in time. He took a breath in hesitation. There was a long pause then he said, "that's a lot of money". I stayed silent. He repeated his statement about it being a lot of money, then asked "am I going to get it back?" I assured him I would give him the money back as soon as I got the insurance or Gerry's checks that were coming. Once again there was a brief silence. I dropped my head wishing I had not called or asked him. I didn't think I would have to beg Gerry's dad to help him. He was a Mason who I'm told took care of their family. Gerry was always there for him. Finally, he said "I can LOAN you three thousand dollars. You're going to pay me back, right?" I again told him I would make sure he got the money back. He told me to have Deborah come pick up a check. I thanked him and we hung up the phone. I could not believe this man, who just had Gerry order over three hundred dollars in cologne online for himself not more than a month before Gerry's death, was this hesitant to help bury his son. Then I thought maybe he was giving me a hard time because Rosa borrowed money from them before when she had trouble and didn't pay them back.

In any case, I picked up the phone and called Tamika back. I told her what transpired with Mister. Then I humbled myself asking if I could borrow one thousand dollars. I would find a way to put together the last thousand. Without hesitation she immediately said, "Yes, I'll bring it to you in the morning?" All I could do was cry. My friend came through when Gerry's family, his flesh was making it so hard. I had not yet made the final decision about who would be at his burial. Yet, I know if I'd asked even two of his close friends, they would have helped financially just like Tee without the struggle I had with Mister.

The funeral home let me know we would lay Gerry to rest on Wednesday. The next morning Tee brought me an envelope with cash as she promised along with an envelope from her mom for me. You appreciate the value of a good friend who is there for you when you need them. Deborah brought me a check from Mister. I collected these funds, adding the thousand I put together and took them to the funeral home to complete paperwork. The balance would be paid later but the space had to be paid for prior to the hand digging of his spot. Next the kids came with me so I could show them where Gerry would be buried as well as pick out a stone marker. All of them seemed ok with where he would be, saying it was nice, including Egypt. That gave me some sense of peace. We drove back with me knowing who in that limited number would be standing for Gerry. We began trying to find and put together family photos we could gather for a collage to stand at the site. In our shock and sadness, we seemed to have come together. It's just sad it took losing Gerry for this to happen.

Once I knew we would bury Gerry Wednesday I only told the kids. I did not have the energy to fight with Gerry's other family members because they all could not be there. It had nothing to do with having to beg for the money to bury him. Though I'm sure in their minds they will look at it that way. Gerry died Sunday, Monday I contacted Mister and it was now Tuesday when I knew who would stand with him the following day.

Rosa tried to reach me, but after Dale's words of death over Gerry, I just couldn't speak with them. I should have known something was up when my girls began getting calls from Rosa and Mister asking questions from them expecting answers that should have come from me. Mister and Rosa never called the girls directly. Rosa never had anything to do with the girls. She never had conversations with them when she did show up to New Jersey outside of hello. And Mister only had dealings with Tinisha if I was unavailable or he needed help on his computer with banking and his accounts since that was her job.

Yet now, Rosa's calling asking them if Gerry had power of attorney over Mister. They all knew Gerry was the one trusted by Mister and Sweety. Gerry was going through the process of preparing Mister's life end paperwork. Mister being one of pride and control could not be rushed in the steps of understanding he needed to have someone look over him as he was aging. His mental state was beginning to slip as well much slower than Sweety. So Gerry was taking his time moving slowly working with his father. Mister had always been the one looking over his own parents long gone. He made the plans for their funerals and property afterwards as the executor. Yet at this time, he couldn't see himself in the position of being the one needing the executor for his own death.

It was difficult for Gerry as well, facing one day his parents will be gone. It was something he didn't want to think of planning for. Still, Mister shared things with Gerry as Gerry spent time with him going through what he had and would leave behind. Mister had several guns throughout the home that were loaded. Gerry unloaded them for safety. With Sweety having dementia and Mister forgetting some things, the last thing wanted is an accident with one of the guns going off. This made Gerry unsettled. He needed his brothers to help. They were always on the receiving end the few times Mister had something to give them all, but had nothing in return to provide be it time or physical object to support their aging parents. I could sympathize with them to a degree of how they felt seeing more of the picture. They were still all of their parents, not just Gerry's. He was at a crossroad and we're now in a pandemic. Just six months to a year earlier we, with our girls, cleaned his parents house top to bottom as it was becoming a state of emergency. Feeling alone in this with only the help of the girls and me, he began steps not only to complete his retirement papers but also go on FMLA to have time to take care of his parents beyond what we were already doing. There was nothing else we could do.

Rosa also wanted to know from the girls if Gerry had a will. Neither of these things should have been of their concern. It was none of their business. They have been absent for thirty years for the most part. She was on a fishing mission with nothing to do with care for anyone but herself. My focus was on getting through laying Gerry to rest at that moment. I didn't have time or care to dissect Rosa's motives. I was just trying to get through one day at a time as painful as it was. I couldn't focus on what the rest of the family was up to. Though maybe I should have. Still, it was a pandemic with no one to be by our side to be eyes, ears and help us navigate through this process. Gerry nor I cared much about things or money when someone died, we cared about people. That's not the case for everyone. Rosa claimed and cleaned out their grandfather's house when he died while everyone stood by. Gerry and I didn't want anything while watching in disgust as the others said nothing, not wanting to speak up. Gerry only asked about a simple barbeque grill, yet even that she took. I got him a bigger and better one for his birthday. I really didn't understand why she was concerned as to whether Gerry had a will, She wasn't part of our family. Gerry made plans for our family without interfering with any of theirs. He only helped them when needed while planning for our care when he was gone.

The morning of the burial all the kids came to the house; Egypt, Israel, KCJ, Deborah and Tinisha. We all decided to wear Gerry's Eagles hats to unify us, he had so many. It also allowed us to feel him closer to us. Egypt made a touching speech that even though Gerry was gone, we would stay close as family like he wanted. That meant so much after years of hoping and praying we could have a real relationship. We still didn't have pictures together the way we wanted. Egypt put most of those together we could find and print out at the last minute on our way to the cemetery. It was cold in the morning with light rain. We all drove our individual cars to keep the social distance for safety. Tinisha drove with her fiancé, Deborah and I drove together, Egypt was in her car, Israel in his. I'm not sure who KCJ rode with. We were met at the site by Gerry's friends. They drove two to a car as well. George and Kevin rode together, Phil rode with his wife Louise. My pastors, Pastor Woods and Pastor Kevin came as well. It took a while for Gerry to arrive, so we waited. We were all very cold. We were there early, it was almost an hour wait. Gerry was worth it.

The car arrived with Gerry in a bamboo coffin. I went to the car placing my hand on the top of it, still finding it hard to believe he was gone. I could feel all eyes on me. I am much stronger than I look and would not let my children see me break. I had to be strong for them. A cart wheels him around to the hand dug grave. We all gathered around his plot. Each one of us said a few words about Gerry ending with us unitedly reciting the Lord's Prayer. Then his friends, his brothers lifted him off the cart and on ropes lowered Gerry in his bamboo coffin down into the hand dug grave. The funeral director thought it was funny that with all the things we each had to say about Gerry, not one or us mentioned the Eagles. We had a laugh; Gerry was all about the Philadelphia EAGLES. He worked for them at Lincoln Financial Field part time over the last ten years just to be in their atmosphere. He loved it and they loved having him. It didn't matter how cold or hot it could get standing in the stands helping people get to their seats. He was there. When they won the Super Bowl, it was a dream come true for him. He always believed they would win. It was his joy when they won the Superbowl for the first time and he got his own Superbowl ring. He was part of the Eagle family. The Eagles acknowledged him personally in a beautiful news article after his death. As wonderful as all this was, they just were not on the forefront of our minds that day. Gerry was so much bigger than that.

Now that Gerry was at rest, I knew I had to face his family. The following day was Mister's eye appointment. The appointment he was concerned about the day Tinisha called telling him her dad died. I began taking him to his eye appointments after Sweety called me hysterical one day while they were driving home from the eye doctor. She was afraid he was going to drive them head on into an accident. His eyes were dilated and he didn't want to wait. She was trying to get him to pull over but he wouldn't listen. I jumped into my car and headed in the direction they were coming from while staying on the phone convincing her to find a place for him to pull over. They got to a closed down Wawa just before they could get on Route 70. I met them there and drove them home, bringing Mister back to pick up his car later. From then on I took them to their appointments. With Tinisha unable, I was hesitant to take them due to not knowing if I had Covid with Gerry's recent death. But I was the only one who was able to take him.

When I arrived at Gerry's parents' home, I saw the New York plates of Dale's car. Immediately the Lord said, "be quiet and get ready." I exited my vehicle as Dale approached me stating "I was mad at you, but I'm not mad anymore". I just looked at him thinking, "If you drove down here all the way from New York, why am I taking YOUR dad for his eye appointment when I should be in isolation after your brother's death?" But God said, "be quiet", so I did. Instead, I waited for Mister and Sweety to come out to the car. I drove them to their appointments in their vehicle. Dale's whole family was there, wife, daughter, their kids and grandbabies in and out of the house. Some had on masks, some didn't. Their daughter approached me but I put up my hand for her to stay a distance. I didn't want to infect anyone, just in case. I was taking a risk as it was taking Mister and Sweety to the eye appointment. I couldn't understand why they were taking things so lightly and with small children around. Then again with

Abandoned

Mister and Sweety gone for a period of time, it gave Rosa full access to go through the entire house.

I drove Mister and Sweety to the eye doctor waiting outside in the vehicle for them to get done. It would not have been safe for me to go into the building, possibly putting others at risk. While I waited, I texted his brothers letting them know I would meet them back at their parents' house at a designated hour and tell them about Gerry. I was going to explain my reasons for the decisions I made and that they were not meant to hurt them. Mister and Sweety hadn't said much of anything the entire trip to or from the appointment. I returned home after dropping them off to copy materials about Gerry's burial for his brothers and parents. I spoke to the girls letting them know I was going to speak with the family asking if they wanted to come. Egypt knew I was going but said she wasn't coming, I eventually learned why. Tinisha met Deborah and I there. Mister and Sweety remained inside the house. I stood at the side of Mister's vehicle outside with his brothers Dale and Samuel with their wives. I handed Samuel information of where Gerry was buried along with a photo of the bamboo coffin he was placed in. I proceeded to explain to him why their parents and they were not at the burial without telling them what Gerry said. It wasn't personal against them or meant to hurt them. He took the materials quietly while listening.

I also told them I needed them to help with their parents because I could not take care of them by myself without

Gerry. We had been taking care of them for years and Mister recently talked about putting Sweety away. He couldn't handle her dementia. If they couldn't help take care of her they may want to consider an independent living senior space for their parents. He remained quiet though he didn't like me saying I could not do it all. Dale had walked away. They had already begun drinking their norm with grieving I guess it's to be expected.

Rosa had a lot to say as she always did telling me how wrong I was not having their parents and brothers there. She picks now to be about family when she spent little to no time here. The last few months she spent crying and complaining to me on the phone about her disdain for Mister and a little of Sweety along with her complaints of Dale in their marriage. She didn't care if Mister was sick or how weak Sweety was, she felt I should have at least had them there. She did not consider if I drove them there unknowingly being positive of covid it could have resulted in them both getting sick and dying. That would then be my fault. She proceeded to say things about the burial she would only know if she were there and saw it, along with comments about how she knew everything because she knows people. It didn't make sense at first but then I began considering the details she was saying and who would know them. At that point, I realized it had to be Egypt. She was standing off to the side at the burial slightly behind me, she must have recorded it and come to show and tell them her thoughts. That's why she did not want to be there. It was a set up and Egypt was behind it. She had not changed. The speech about us being a close family on the day of Gerry's burial was another performance.

I thought it odd and very hurtful for Rosa to come at me in this manner after months of her calling me frequently in tears over her marriage problems asking for prayer. Through the years of Gerry's and my marriage, she and Samuel's wife frequently talked about me in the negative. Mostly because I was not like them. I grew to be tolerated by them and their spouses, but never embraced as family. As long as I cooked for them when they came to town with a huge feast to not just feed them, but make enough food to take back home, I was fine for the moment. I was their sister, they loved me. Now I'm standing in front of her as she verbally attacks me for following my dead husband's wishes. Still, I heard her out understanding their feelings of rejection based on Egypt's narrative. All this while watching both my daughters facial expressions knowing their protectiveness over me. I explained I was trying to keep Tinisha calm since she was carrying twins.

That's when Samuel's wife said, "is she really having twins? Everybody wants to have twins like me". In annoyance I told her "Yes, she is having twins. I am a twin, and her fiancé has twins in his family too. So YES, she's carrying twins". I could read Tinisha's face that she was getting upset with the verbal attacks on me. Having had enough she said she was going home. I thought that was a good idea, telling her to get some rest. She left while

Deb and I remained. I let Rosa continue with her rant not wanting to cut her off. I began feeling lightheaded knowing I needed to lay down but didn't want to be rude by just walking away in the middle of Rosa's complaining. I can't understand why they were so upset not being able to stand over Gerry's grave when they were never there for anything celebrating his life while he was here.

I began seeing a dark halo tunnel vision. I needed to get out of there but I was trying to let her finish venting. I finally could not hold out any longer telling Deborah I was going to faint. Leaning against the car, I dropped to the ground while Rosa was speaking. She screamed briefly calling for one of the men nearby to help me to my car. Someone, I learned later was Samuel; tried to pull me up while I was still dizzy, dark and with no focus. I told them to not touch me, give me a minute. They took offense to that. It wasn't personal, I just needed my head to stop spinning for a minute before I moved. They let me go. Rosa told one of the boys to help me to the car. None of them did.

Deborah got me to the car telling me she was taking me to the hospital. When I got there, they were unable to draw blood. I was extremely dehydrated. The hospital admitted me Covid positive, my kidneys were not functioning properly. My kidneys were also the first thing affected when I had toxic shock syndrome. Covid must have latched onto this once weak area in my body. Thankfully,

Abandoned

I was only in the hospital overnight. I received another word along with the "get ready" I received the day of the confrontation. This time to "block them from my social media" from whatever was going to happen next. I did not know what and would never have believed it if anyone had told me. I knew they were mad but never imagined this.

I was quarantined at home in my room for thirty days. Deborah took care of me, leaving food at the door. I'm thankful the Lord shielded her. She never got Covid in all that time. I didn't know how I would pay the bills, how to find the life insurance information, social security, I had not heard back from workers comp either after Gerry died. I was lost. But God. Gerry's job had planned a drive by parade for me the day I ended up in the hospital. When they got word of my hospital admission and it had to be canceled, they sent an envelope to my home. They brought me cards with money, and my church connected me with people who could help me with social security and other financial directions.

Gerry had additional paychecks come in allowing me to quickly write a check paying Mister his three thousand dollars back. I took my friend Tee back her loan in the same manner she gave it to me. Gerry received a large vacation check that covered his burial expenses where he ended up burying himself. Even though Gerry's family was understandably upset. There was not one call of comfort from his family. The only exception was Sweety.

She called daily with the mothers cry. She repeated the same thing each time she called, "I lost my son, my good son, the one who never gave me any problems." My heart went out to her, unable to comfort her since I was in the same pain over the same loss. She also cried "now she knows how it feels to lose your child" again as much as I loved her, I could only listen but so much. She didn't know how it felt to lose her spouse she deeply loved. Beyond Gerry's death, she didn't know or understand all the things her family were doing behind the scenes. She really had no comprehension of taking care of bills like she used to or understanding details in paperwork or letters. Her short term memory was in and out.

They contributed nothing toward Gerry's burial. Mister made it clear the money I asked for was a loan to be repaid. After all Gerry did throughout his life to carry and take care of them. He wasn't worth their financial support in death? This was his family, the one he didn't want me to find out about or see. I texted Israel to see if he was alright. He had been talking with me prior to and just after the burial. He called me mom. We never had problems with our relationship. At times I was closer to Israel than to KCJ. When others in their family saw the faults in Israel, I could see there was good in him even when he acted up. He was a sensitive, emotional young man, like his uncle Roman. Unfortunately, alcohol was his coping mechanism. When he drank he was out of control. But when he wasn't drinking, he was a very nice young man. This time I got back two words, "not really". Then he stopped responding to me altogether. I didn't know what happened. I still wasn't aware of everything going on between Egypt, Rosa and Mister. Prior, he and Egypt had not been on speaking terms for over a year with legal issues between them. She had wished him dead more times than I recall. I did not associate Egypt's new betrayal of or towards me as having anything to do with why I had not heard from Israel.

On Father's Day, I learned Egypt began writing horrible posts about me on social media trying to discredit my character. She told the truth about Gerry's family not being at his burial but without the facts or reasons why. She called me toxic as an insult in reference to me having survived toxic shock syndrome which created my disability. Therefore, the Lord forewarned me to "block them". Thankfully I had not seen the post directly until I was able to see Gerry's Facebook page. I saw her post insulting me while posting photos of herself as a baby with him. She was in pain, yes, this I could understand but not the personal attacks or comments of how she wishes they could go back to the days when it was just the two of them together. He was her father, not her man. I deleted her post. Gerry hated Facebook and this was something his friends did not need to see. Gerry did his best to hide the division with his daughter and me. He would have hated it. However, I did not block her from his page at the time. She had the right to grieve for her dad. I did not want to take that away. I hoped she would see the reason, but she continued to post things to attack me and post photos of her and her mom on his page giving me no other choice than to block her and other family members from his page. They have the right to grieve posting their hatred of me any way they want on their personal social media pages if that is what they so choose to do. But doing it creates an embarrassment in Gerry's memory I was not going to allow. Not on his page. Our entire life together I did what I had to protect him, his heart and his public image. They could not realize as they insulted who I am, they were also saying he was stupid to be with me. Gerry was not a stupid man. He was the smartest man I know. Much more than anyone in his family. He loved me, I loved him and when I agreed to marry him, it was in spite of whatever hell his family, most specifically Egypt brought into my life. I would always guard him and his reputation. When she wasn't posting on social media, she was contacting our daughters telling them what a horrible mother I was trying to turn them against me. When that didn't work, she wished death on Tinisha's yet unborn twins. The girls tried to stay neutral at first by listening and giving Egypt and Israel a chance to air their grievances against me. There is no way they would turn their back on me for them. They wouldn't turn their backs on their own mother. The girls tried to explain they, Egypt and Israel, did not know what Gerry and I discussed as a married couple. It fell on deaf ears with more insults. Ultimately, the girls stopped communicating with them altogether.

While all this was going on, Sweety got even worse. She was grieving so hard, calling four and five times crying over Gerry losing the son that mattered the most for her, "good son", "the one who never gave her any trouble". I wanted to be there for her. If it had not been Gerry I would have been able to comfort her in her hour of grief. But I was in my own grief losing the one man I ever really loved while watching for social media attacks and keeping our daughters calm during it. She was out of her mind with grief telling me I don't know what it feels like to lose your child. I didn't and prayerfully never will. She too didn't know how it felt to lose her spouse. We loved one another and both in our own deep grief in this loss were unable to comfort the other.

Mister told Deborah to tell me he wanted a copy of Gerry's death certificate. I did not understand why he didn't call and talk to me directly like he's always done. He'd call me to set the clock in his car, put together cheap gadgets he bought or other things out of the blue. Along with when to take him to his appointments. Why he wasn't calling now was lost to me. Something didn't feel right. I decided if he wanted a copy, he could call me directly. I had gotten the state letter for Gerry's life insurance and pension. Gerry made me and the girls aware he had life insurance three times his salary, some three hundred thousand dollars so we would be well taken care of if he died. I didn't want to hear that. I wanted Gerry. Still, he insisted we knew. His parents knew as well, especially Mister. I'm sure his brothers were probably aware too. They knew how hard Gerry worked all his life to make sure his family was provided for. It now made sense why no one in his family was happy about him getting married.

As long as Gerry was alone, everything he had worked for went to his family, including his life insurance. With me getting gravely ill early in our marriage and his trust of Sweety in case anything happened to me; he had us both named on the policy as primary. Secondly he listed, in order, KCJ, Egypt and Israel. Our girls had not been born yet. He did not have Mister at all. I was not aware of the details on the policy at the time. I saw no need to look at it. I wasn't sure where it was at first. We had not gotten deep in discussing our end life plans. Gerry did tell our daughter Tinisha he had to take their grandmother off the policy along with the K.P. 's to add our girls. Now with her dementia, Gerry was working to get Sweety off the policy because she was no longer of sound mind to stand for the children or me, and I now was much better. She no longer needed to be on the policy. Trying to get through to the state with the shutdown was a challenge with long hold times, along with all the other things he was trying to accomplish. He died before he could complete his tasks. That allowed for evil intentions and greed to step in. That was the reason for Rosa's call to find out if Gerry had a life insurance policy that would block what they planned.

Rosa had already begun plotting to see what she could take now that Gerry was out of the way. She could not stand up against him. He would not tolerate it and the other brothers were weak. They let her say and do what she wanted. When my quarantine was over, I took food to Sweety and Mister. Mister had just driven home. I was speaking with Sweety on the porch still masked, keeping a distance. Then Mister walked past me into the house without speaking. After he passed by me, he stopped in the living room, turning to me saying, "did Debbie tell you I want a copy of the death certificate?" I asked him why he wanted the death certificate. He must have felt challenged by his response. He had an expression of "how dare I question him" on his face. I should just do as he says. He replied, "for my records". He followed with "if you don't give it to me, I can get one on my own". I just looked at him thinking something wasn't right. I didn't understand why he was acting as he was. I thought of him as a father for the thirty years I was with Gerry. Now he is treating me as a stranger. Almost attacking me, the one who is still here trying to help them, with their sons nowhere in sight.

I wanted to find out why Mister was now treating me so coldly. One Sunday the first lady spoke saying an apology can change things if someone is offended. I thought about Mister, maybe I offended him in a way beyond that I am unaware I decided after church to speak with him. I drove to their home after church, finding him on the front porch of his home. I apologized for anything I did to offend him with Gerry dying. It is here I learned he felt he should have controlled what went on for Gerry's burial, all planning and arrangements. He didn't feel me as his wife had the right to make the plans. He felt as his father I should have stepped aside to allow him to do things the way he felt they should be done. He had taken care of the other funerals of his family members. Being his wife had nothing to do with it. He questioned the fact that neither he nor his family gave anything to help toward Gerry's burial. Stating "didn't we give money to help with Gerry". I reminded him by his words, he loaned me money and I gave it back to him. So no, he nor any of the family contributed anything towards Gerry's death. Miscommunication gave him the impression that the pastors discussed and arranged Gerry's service. I don't know if he received this information as untrue as it was from Egypt and her narrative of the burial or just rumors fed between Rosa and Egypt. I explained the pastors had only met that day. Which was true. Pastor Woods and Pastor Kevin met for the first time in person at Gerry's grave. I made the arrangements the little there was.

He was upset and for good reason he and his family were not there. They didn't consider most things in Gerry's life, they were not there. He asked, "did Gerry say he didn't want us there". I explained it was for his and Sweety's health not being there. If their health had been better at the time, it would have been different. They would have been there. I wanted them to be there. I may have been able to find a way to make it work if the situation wasn't so dire. I told him "No, Gerry never said he didn't want you there". I didn't explain about the brothers. In truth, Gerry didn't want them there, but they would not understand or believe that. They surely would not believe it coming from his wife, they tolerated but never fully accepted into the family. Mister didn't respect me as Gerry's wife to handle his death. In the past he didn't think much of his daughters-in-law's by helping in situations when he could. Having one with the ability to handle things without him was an insult. He was used to everyone answering to his command or leaving them stranded on their own, expecting them to fail. He didn't take into consideration the circumstances. If it were not for the pandemic, I would have talked with him about Gerry's and my plans. He still would not have been in charge. Gerry still would have been buried as he was, but Mister would have known more details and be part of it prior. Then he told me Sweety got a letter for Gerry's life insurance. I was confused. Now it was clear why he wants the death certificate and would get it without me. He wanted the money and could not get it without the documents.

I went to see my friend Tee who is an attorney telling her what was going on. When I showed her the insurance information from the state, she told me "B, based on the county life insurance this is not Gerry's total earnings, it looks like half." She told me I could go online and see what he earned. In the thirty years we were married I never bothered to find out what he made. I had no need. He took care of us and that was all that mattered. I trusted him. In any case she was right. The amount I was to receive in the letter was half of what Gerry told us it was. As I talked to Tee, knowing Gerry too, she reminded me about my illness and why he probably still had her on the policy. That made sense with Gerry's order of doing things. Also, with Gerry telling Tinisha he was trying to get Sweety off the policy before he died. I figured all I had to do is go back to Mister and Sweety to let them know what happened. The policy was not meant for Sweety to receive but entrusted that we would be taken care of with it if anything happened. I expected them to be reasonable, we are family. I expected Mister to be reasonable, given all Gerry and I have done for them knowing our household status without Gerry.

Mister and Sweety, late in their years, were well situated with large bank accounts and pensions in addition to their social security and life insurance policies. They had secure finances, they didn't need what Gerry meant for us. Sweety didn't know why she got the policy and was not in the state of mind to make any decisions about it. Mister clammed up saying he didn't know what she was going to do with it. This was followed by him asking me "do you know Gerry's social security number?" At that point, I knew he had no intention of giving the kids and me the other half of Gerry's life insurance and pension. He would show Sweety, who had no understanding of what she was signing and where, in order to get the money himself. In response to him asking me if I knew Gerry's social security number, I told him "Yes I know it", and I

Abandoned

walked away, got in my car and drove home. I was not going to help him rob my family.

At this point Mister knew very well what he was doing. He knew the right thing to do but chose the path to not only take from me and his grandchildren but even more, take from the son who looked after him when the others did not. I was angry and hurt. It was about more than the money. This was a family I thought I belonged to. It was a family I stood by at times my own family wanted me to be with them. Rosa and Dale would barely come to Camden before. When Sweety broke her hip, they had no time to come help as I drove Mister to the hospital and rehab twice a day for weeks as well as cook for them. Now they stayed swarming around because there was money coming. While Gerry was alive Rosa could not control the narrative. Without Gerry there, she could run the show because none of the other men stood up to her. She was now once again in position as favorite daughter with me out of the way.

Mister got the documents he needed on his own over time, so the insurance and pension was legally released to Sweety, well over one hundred thousand dollars. Had she been in her right mind it would not have happened. She is a woman of integrity like her son. I believe Sweety would have given the funds back to me for the kids. Another victim, they took advantage of her illness for their greed. I was told I should seek out a lawyer to try and recover at least part of the money considering the situation.

Sweety was not capable of making decisions nor acting in her own right on the policy. Outsiders were claiming the policy since Gerry had no will and I had no document stating Gerry's clear intentions for his life insurance. The simple fact is I, as his wife and his mother with dementia, should carry some weight in court. As I thought about it I decided not to. Gerry always said his sanity and peace of mind was more valuable than anything. That is so true. I wasn't going to fight over stolen money, when I knew it belonged to me and our children. If it takes over one hundred thousand dollars to get evil out of my life, it's worth the cost.

No sooner than the check cleared Dale and Rosa moved Mister and Sweety to New York to live with them. This way now Rosa has control over not only Mister and Sweety's finances, including life insurance; but she has Gerry's money too. The sadder part is Sweety didn't like Rosa or want to be around her before the dementia, now she will end her days away from her close friends and loved ones to be with the one person she didn't want to be with. It's a terrible thing to be moved out of your environment away from everyone you have known all your life when you are in your eighties. The last place you want to be at that age is living in a house with screaming little children. I felt bad for them. At least for Sweety who talked about the noise all the time when talking on the phone with Rosa when she did. As I look at it, they didn't take money from me or Gerry and my children at all. They took what should have gone to Egypt and Israel. Gerry had four children, cutting the policy in half meant they took their inheritance. Egypt in her actions of attacking me helped them do it by not one of them standing up to the situation. They simply helped Rosa outsmart them to take what was theirs.

I had hoped to have peace with them even after they abandoned my family and stole the insurance but that was not going to happen. I tried to accept the fact the girls and I were completely on our own. Still, I loved and missed Sweety. I used to talk to her almost every day with me telling her "I love you". She'd answer, "I love you, more" and I say, "I love you most" and hang up. With Gerry gone she was not herself at all. Everyone was stressed out knowing her condition while trying to cope with our own grief. In all the years I've known Sweety I only heard her curse once. It was during this time of Gerry's passing and the dementia getting worse before moving to New York. She called one of her multiple times like she did. She'd been calling one of the girls too. She was upset that my daughter was not calling her back. When I explained she was having difficulty coping, Sweety got really angry, cursed and hung up the phone. It both shocked and hurt me. I should have understood but couldn't even bring myself to call her at the time. When she did call me later, she didn't remember doing it.

Rosa remained with them by this time making sure I didn't have contact with her now that the money was secure. I could no longer talk to Sweety as I did. After moving them away, I could not reach her at all. You must go through Rosa who was jealous of our relationship and would not let me talk to her if I were to ask. I amount it to being just short of a hostage situation. Rosa controlling who she talks to and when because Sweety's memory was failing with little memory of basic numbers she used to know to reach anyone on her own. Over time she would not know me at all, the only thing I know Rosa would enjoy.

Since I couldn't talk to her, I sent Sweety a card from the girls and me for Mother's Day. I received a phone call the Friday before Mother's Day. It was Rosa on the phone. She asked, "Did you send a Mother's Day card here?" I told her "Yes". She proceeded to tell me "Don't contact them, don't send any cards, letters, or anything else. They don't want to have anything to do with you...." I said ok and hung up the phone while she was still ranting. It was hurtful of course. Not only did we lose Gerry, my husband and our daughter's father. We lost an entire family. She now made it plain without question of doubt. I had to tell the girls about the call so they too would understand. One of them is more protective of me and my feelings than the other, not wanting to have anything to do with them at all. This is along with things they did and said directly to her. The other only feels hurt yet tries to stay neutral not knowing what to say when she runs into someone who knew we were family, but not anymore. It was a big blow that only my heavenly Father, Abba, my BaBa could understand as I cried out to him once again wishing all this didn't have to happen. Gerry was the foundational glue that held everything together on this side of heaven for our family. Everything fell apart when he earned his wings. I didn't know what the outcome would be.

About two weeks later, I received word that Mister died suddenly. Or rather he had a massive stroke and was brain dead on life support. I contacted Roman who said he knew and was headed to Dale's to make decisions. When I heard, I had no joy, but I also had no sorrow regarding his passing. That bothered me. I didn't understand why I was unmoved by his death. I was experiencing more sadness for my pastor's family whose dog had just died. This was not like me. I loved Mister like a father at one time, but now that he is gone, I feel nothing. I went to my Father asking God why I am not feeling any sadness for his life ending. I was directed to Exodus 22:22-27 *"Do not take advantage of the widow or the fatherless. If you do and they cry out to me, I will certainly hear their cry. My anger will be aroused, and I will kill you with the sword; your wives will become widows and your children fatherless."* (NIV) I froze as I read those words. I did cry out to God with all they had done, Mister being the head of the household. It was God's will after I tried to do what was right only to be met again and again with insult and attack. I didn't wish death for Mister the way Egypt casually wishes it on family members with no remorse. I never thought his life would end as it did. You would also think now that they have everything they want to take, that any division would end. But no, not with them. Not yet.

They brought Mister back to Camden so he could have the Mason funeral he wanted. They were able to have a full funeral and burial unlike Gerry since many pandemic restrictions had ended, though it seems Covid will never go away. In Mister's obituary they mention Gerry as a son deceased. There is no mention of him having a wife or children. It states Mister had two daughters in laws, Rosa and Samuel's wife. They completely cut our existence out of their lives. I had never heard of anything like that in my life. It only shows the depth of their disdain for Gerry's and my relationship. Was it so terrible that their son chose to have love in his life with a wife, children and happiness? Most parents want that for their children. I know I do. Their dislike of me being different, strong, independent with ability, not conforming to living as they did created greed and evil intentions in their heart. This was their choice to take the path they took. Everything was under their control, so they thought. They have yet to realize God has true control. Thy kingdom come; thy will be done.

Forgive

"If you forgive those who sin against you, your heavenly Father will forgive you. But if you refuse to forgive others, your Father will not forgive your sins."

As I said in the opening of the last chapter, there are no bad people. From the beginning of the word in Genesis, it clearly states at the end of each day of creation; *"and God saw that it was good."* When He created man with instruction of his purpose and ability on the sixth and last day of creation in Genesis 1:31 *"Then God looked over all of us, we are more than good, we are in His words very good!"* (NLT). So when God made us, all of us, we are more than good, we are in His words very good.

You may think with everything said and done prior, in abandoned, how do you go from good to that. The simple answer is choice. The Lord loves us enough to give us the choice to follow Him and continue to do good and right. Or we have the choice to follow our own mind and direction according to what pleases us. It may not please the Lord, but it's not like He hasn't faced it before and the reason some of us choose the paths we do today.

Lucifer was God's prized worshiper created with jewels and music within him to reflect God's majesty with praise. However, somewhere along the line, pride and jealousy took over within him causing him to feel he was the one who should be worshiped and praised. He no longer wanted to be the reflection of God. He wanted to be God. God wasn't having that. I'm not sure about all households, but in many homes, if the child feels like they no longer must listen to or obey their parents disrupting the entire home, it's time for them to go. On a job, if you tell the supervisor, you will do things the way you want, your way and he or she must deal with it, that position will not be yours for very long. This is where Lucifer went off script. He tried to prove his point by bringing other angels on board with his belief. Their attempt at a coup over heaven failed miserably with Lucifer and his angel cohorts being kicked out of heaven. Lucifer's name which meant "Morning Star" was even taken from him, changing to "Satan", accuser, or adversary. Now his bitterness is focused to steal, kill and destroy everything that God created good.

That brings us back to the actions of people. Standing alone, we are weak. The forces of darkness are so strong, if we do not fill ourselves with the light of Jesus which gives us power to fight, we will fall. We must walk in the light that is our strength, keeping us strong to avoid the control of darkness.

Abandoned speaks the facts of events that happened after Gerry's passing. They are told not to discredit those written about. Their names were changed to not point them out directly as it is clear they do not want to be recognized as a part of my life. Their identity is known only to those who personally know me and the family. Abandoned also is not written to make myself appear to be an innocent victim. The truth is simply the truth. It is something we sometimes don't want to face, especially if we are wrong. Sometimes pride won't let us acknowledge our wrongdoings. It's like catching a glance at our crime in a mirror, then walking away quickly before being seen. But if we stand up and face our fear of standing alone against the group to do the right thing, we'll gain greater respect for ourselves and from others.

While reading Abandoned, you may have felt angry at spots of sadness causing you to feel a heaviness in your chest. That's what anger does, it's the darkness of Satan creeping in. That heaviness makes it hard to breathe and even harder to have joy; true joy. We can walk around acting like we are happy in front of others while in truth there is a sadness holding us back. It is a weight we are not meant to carry and the only way to get rid of it is through forgiveness. Forgiveness is the wings that set us free for flight. It lets us soar above everything we have experienced that has caused us pain or disappointment. Forgiveness is healing. But how do we get there? How did I get there? And yes, I have forgiven them, all of them and I wish no harm to them. It's not for me to judge them by any of their actions.

I did not always feel this way walking through Abandoned. It took me a LOT of prayer, listening and understanding that everyone has a backstory I have no complete knowledge of. As I reflect on Egypt, through her eyes I invaded her perfect life. She was living with her dad as the only important female in his life. She was his first born and a girl. She had him wrapped around her finger for her every desire. It was alright for him to have some girlfriends if she did not consider a permanent role in his life. As a child she didn't have the mind to consider he may have been lonely for a permanent companion to fill his life someday. She couldn't see it could never take away the love he has for her. By the time she realized I was more than someone he was seeing for the moment, it only gave her cause to find a way to push me out of his life. Maybe if she frustrated me enough, she would cause me to break up with Gerry. That way she would again have him all to herself. She needed to be the center of her dad's world. It almost happened, but Gerry wouldn't let it.

I on the other hand was a new mother of a five year old with no clue of the thoughts or mind of a teenager. I was looking forward to having a girl in my life. I thought it would be an easy thing, his kids and my child getting along. I only thought of blending together the perfect family with two parents who loved their children. Her cold silence made me unsure with no way to break the ice. Gerry suggested I take her to my apartment to help me with some things to bond. That didn't work. We rode in silence the twenty minute drive to Pine Hill where she was expected to help with chores. Unknowingly, it put me in the position of wicked step-mother from the start. In return I got clothes ruined. I was not brought up going to the beauty shop getting my hair and nails done. Had that been something I was used to doing, I would have thought about taking her to lunch and the salon instead. But in all honesty I was lost as to how to form a relationship with her. She was bold and loud, I was timid and soft spoken. It was not for lack of trying, and trying and trying again and again. I kept trying for several reasons. I don't like to fail, she was Gerry's daughter so I wanted to get along with her to make him happy and I always wanted a daughter. Each time it seemed I was getting close, she showed me it was just an illusion. Still, each time she asked something of me whether it was to repair something she was wearing or make the house available to her for her daughters' proms I said yes, preparing as I would have for my own daughters. Gerry saw how much her rejections hurt me through the years until he told me "I can't make her respect you, don't do anything for her for my sake. Tell her no." It truly did boil down to respect. That was the first time I felt like I had a choice to not do for Egypt without breaking the promise I made in my heart to put up with whatever I had to face from his family because I love him.

These last actions from her creating the division in what was our family, wishing death on my unborn grandbabies is something I don't want to come back from. I forgive her. I have to. If I didn't forgive her, she would have further control over my life. I don't think she is a bad person. I still care about her, but not enough to want her as part of my life anymore. She is a little girl crying out for her daddy in an adult body. Forgiveness frees me of that moment in time she took from me and keeps her from holding me hostage in bitterness. I pray someday she finds her own healing and even more, salvation in Christ.

Israel was a troubled child for a long time. He lived in Egypt's shadow walking in her footsteps doing what she said. He got in trouble often, I believe it was his way to get attention. Or just bad timing. He always seemed to be in the wrong place at the wrong time. It may also be from something he experienced unsaid as a child. I never had much of a problem with him from all his outbursts through the years. Had I known the hidden secret of one thing he had done, it would have been very different. He never directly disrespected me in the way Egypt had, though he impacted KCJ's life with negative energy.

When Gerry passed, after Egypt went into action, he chose to believe and follow her actions in a more subdued way. He chose to spread verbal rumors to neighbors on my street of how I turned my back on them and left them out. He was also demanding to anyone who would listen, (not to me) he should have all of Gerry's watches and cologne as his only son. He did not consider KCJ. He hasn't lived on the street in years and caused problems when he did. Thankfully most of my neighbors saw him for who he is paying him no attention.

He is a hurting son. The only biological son of his father. He spent little time with Gerry nor listened to the advice Gerry tried to give him for the direction of his life. Now

Gerry is gone. His pain is guilt for what he should have done. Both Egypt and Israel have guilt for not spending more time with the amazing father they had and not letting him spend time with his grandchildren and great grands the way he should have been able too. I feel sorry for Israel who still needs guidance and direction. Being angry and bitter with him would be like pouring more salt onto a wound. I want him to gain his life and become the man his father wanted him to be. The things he said about me to discredit my character are minor. He needs to find within himself the man he is truly meant to be. If my prayers and forgiveness can make that happen I know I'm doing the will of God.

Roman didn't really say or do anything to offend or cause me pain. There is really nothing to forgive. He just stayed absent which is how he usually is. He's always stayed away from the mess. A part of me saw him as a victim himself. When he was young and doing well Mister was proud of him. It seemed that he fell in love, things changed with hard choices he made putting him on the outs. It seemed Mister never saw him in the same way. Without forgiveness and support of the family Roman never was able to again achieve the things he once had. I would like to see him as a brother. It's just unfortunate he is caught in the frays of his family. Then again, if you don't stand up for something, you'll fall for anything. If you're not a part of the solution, you are part of the problem. He neither stood with them in their actions, nor told them they were wrong making me unable to trust or communicate with him. I like Roman and am sorry we will no longer be family. I offer my forgiveness to him for all that has been lost and for his not standing for Gerry.

Samuel was the oldest but in many ways the weakest. Unlike Gerry, his younger brother, he did not stand up and speak when something was wrong. He had little control over his own family therefore he could not be expected to stand up for anyone else. While Rosa and Mister plotted he remained silent. Perhaps if he stayed silent he could secure a comfortable future for his family and himself. It worked for a little while. He and his family moved into Mister's house when they were transported to New York. But only months after Samuel lost his wife, Rosa got a good offer to sell the house telling him and his family they all had to leave. Rosa may have had some reasons for selling the home, but no compassion for displacing them the way she did while he was still in a grieving state. Samuel never did anything directly to my family with the exception of his silent support of what was done. I can forgive that and have. My heart goes out to him for his loss regardless of how his wife treated or felt about me. I hope he finds rest and peace with his family.

When I consider Israel, Roman and Samuel I think of the words in Ephesians 4:32 *"be kind to each other, tenderhearted, forgiving one another, just as God through Christ has forgiven you"* (NLT). Forgiveness has given me the ability to be kind to them if in their presence, even though that is unlikely. They were neither captain nor co-captain, only players on the team.

Mister, Dale and Rosa are a different story and different level of forgiveness I had to dig down deep to reach. Dale speaking death over Gerry's life rather than simply praying, then being mad at me about the situation showed his self centeredness. If he took one millisecond to put his own wife or child in my place, I'm sure his heart and actions would have been different. At least I hope. If not for a major family celebration, his mothers birthday or parents' anniversary, the only time he would come to Camden is when Gerry and I had something planned to include them. It was never just to come see his parents, his brother or see how he could help or be of support to his family. When he got here, he had time to drink and cut up with loud jokes talking about people. They came with empty pockets when it came to giving, but left with hands full.

Mister and Rosa have personalities that are very much alike. Both of them like to be the center of attention, they are controlling, prideful and money hungry. They are clearly the definition of a word I don't like, narcissist. They have an unreasonably high sense of their own importance. They need and seek too much attention and want people to admire them. They lack the ability to understand and care about others in their true state. They are effective at acting out care and concern but are actually just a mirage.

Dale may have married Rosa because subconsciously, she reminded him of Mister wanting the love and respect of his father. Rosa was able to manipulate and control the other boys. Gerry she could not. The moment she learned of Gerry's death was like blood in the water, her being the shark circling above waiting to strike. She will put on a presence of caring for family and doing for them only to see what she can get in return. She's similar to Egypt, only Egypt hadn't reached the level of deception for monetary gain as she. Otherwise she would not have let Rosa get away with taking her inheritance. Mister expected everyone to come to him for his advice as the only one with answers, as though he was the GodFather. I thought of him as my dad in the absence of my own being part of my life. Anytime he called me I was there. I began making homemade soup just because he liked soup he got from the diner, but it was too salty. I also want to keep his diabetes in check. When Sweety broke her hip I was his full time on call driver. His turning on me in the way he did was a massive temper tantrum followed by greed taking from his son in order to try to hurt me for not submitting to his will. How arrogant could one man be? And yes, it hurt. The second father figure to leave my life.

He took pride in being a 33rd Degree Mason, people looked up to him. That position was one who is to take care of his son and family of a son, from what I'm told. Instead he turned his back and tried to cause harm in the worst possible way. Gerry nor I cared much for the mason order. Gerry never wanted to be one. We cared about him. So we went to every banquet to support him. Not to speak ill of the now departed, his life had value. However, his actions showed me how right our thoughts and opinions of the organization or at least his position in it are. In the end, no man or organization stands above the only living God. I believe Mister truly just did not want any of his sons to have a happy life or marriage. That was the one major thing Gerry did wrong. He married and found love creating a family built on the foundation of Christ.

Though she'd call me crying, asking for prayer over Dale's indiscretions, Rosa was only too happy to assist in what she perceived was taking from me. She didn't like what Gerry and I had together and she didn't like Mister. Pairing with him in his weakened state, she looked at the prize ahead with his early signs of dementia too and possible impending death with diabetes. It would all be hers. I say hers because she neither thought much of Dale with the problems and she wore the pants in their house. Forgiving their evil plotting was the most difficult. Their action raised an anger in me I'd never felt. They weren't just attacking me, they were attacking and taking from my children. The one way to make a lioness roar is to mess with her cubs. My anger was blood red fire unlike anything I ever felt in my entire life. I kept trying to think of how Gerry would have dealt with the situation. I know he was not happy with his brothers prior to his death and we both were protective of our children. Even when Gerry was upset with someone he had a way of containing his anger even when his entire paycheck was taken by his brother. If Gerry could do it, I had to find my way through it too.

Again to God I went telling His everything He already knew about how I felt. He took me back to Epheians 4:31 *"Let all bitterness, wrath, anger, clamor, and evil speaking be put away from you, with all malice. And be kind to one another;.."* I have been able to let go of the bitterness I've felt. The taste was horrible in my mouth. The wrath I felt was like iron chains or a mountain on my back too heavy to carry. It had to be dropped. Malice, the intention or desire to do evil; ill will. I have none. It's only money, a lot of money yes, but I will not let it be the root of evil in my life. It's no longer important to me. That in itself lets me know that God has taken over to remove that part within me. There is an empty space where love used to be. Erased from existence. That is the sad part. I don't know how kind I can be to these people. For real, that has been a struggle, they hurt my babies. They took from my babies. Gerry knew I would have taken care of and seen that ALL our children had everything he meant for them no matter what. His family took that away from them. It was a LOT to forgive, but just like the extreme pain of labor that vanishes immediately after giving birth, God is able to warm the heart to forgive again. I am praying asking God to prepare me should I encounter them to let me meet them with the kindness He requires. In the meantime, I hope I don't see them again.

Forgive

As I reflect back on many things in my life I remain still waiting to see what emotion is drawn from inside of me. I think back to my earliest memories of trauma that stifled my childhood and how I have gotten through it. How have I handled those triggers keeping me in a holding place? One of them being molested as a child and those things that followed that should and should not have happened. When I came to full understanding of the complete picture being able to stand and confront those who halted my planned development the glass was broken. There was no longer a hold on me. In that case, I was able to make amends and currently have a relationship with them. Though the close bond that should have and could have been won't be re-established. We were able to accept and forgive. It's a relationship I am still rebuilding. I have love for that person who was under the power and control of something greater than them at the time. God told me it was time and showed me how to forgive with my whole heart. I'm not going to say things are perfect like good old times. Things will never be the way they could have been "if". Yet we can't live in a world of what "if's". What I know is, the fear of being in a small space with that person is gone. They have paid their own cost for their life actions just as I've had to pay for my own.

As a young adult, those words that echoed in my ears each time I looked in the mirror took away my self confidence and worth, no longer trigger me. I no longer see her in the mirror. I see and hear the words of my Father in Psalm 139:14 *"I will praise thee; for I am fearfully and wonderfully made: marvelous are thy works; and that my soul knoweth right well".* The words and voice of Jekalyn Carr's song "Bigger" ring loudly in my ear. There is nothing bigger than God, there are no words greater. The enemy is an opposer who will say I am something I am not. I just keep listening to the voice of God. Molestation, emotional, physical, mental abuse, sickness, betrayal or even death; there is nothing bigger or greater than God who will bring you through it if you trust Him. If you truly want to get over something. In the words of my Gerry Baker, L. I. G. it!; Let It Go! It's possible.

In some situations, the relationship will be restored. That is a wonderful thing. In other situations it may not be, you will go your separate way down separate paths not meant to journey together again. That is a good thing also. What is most important is for you to follow the steps to the road God meant for you to become everything you were meant to be. In that way, you will reach more people than you can dream. You have now become fruitful to multiply as in God's original plan when He made us.

I don't know if I will ever re-establish any kind of relationship with my husband's people ever again. It's my personal desire not to. They have already given me over thirty years of trauma and triggers. I think that's enough. I can finally breathe again at ease. But in the end, it's not up to me. It's up to God. I don't know His plans. What I know is He freed me with His love and patience allowing me to get through it all coming full circle becoming resilient. I've experienced love like none other and loss none so deep. I've been abandoned unlike any other and learned to forgive on a higher plain. That's God. He took away the pain. It feels really good to not have any bitterness in my heart. That's real freedom and true joy. In all things, let your light shine so men and women can see the good in you. God's good in you lets you know that all things work together for the good of those who love God and called for His purpose. May God bless and keep you, may He shine His light down on you and give you peace.

Conclusion

I heard a pastor once say there are demonic people living among us. I thought about those words and I'm not sure if I agree. Or at least I have not met or run into a demonic person that I know of. The definition of "demonic" on the internet states it as resembling or characteristic of demon or evil spirits, fiercely energetic, frenzied, diabolic, fiendish.

I have experienced some pretty ugly things said and done to me in my life. This one by Gerry's family being the worst. Some may consider them to be or have acted in a demonic manner. I don't. I look at them as being lost. Things they did were pure evil for evil's sake, that had nothing to do with grief. Does that make them demonic? I say no. It just makes them mean or heartless. They saw it as an opportunity and they took it not caring who they hurt in the path or how they dishonored the wishes or memory of their loved one in death.

Theirs is a symptom of society as a whole without Christ. It is a me first society. Get what I want, when I want, the way I want, how I want and I'll knock down anyone who gets in my way to get it. Then I dare you to say something about it. It is all very sad. I can almost hear the Lord crying. In their case, it is not as though they did not have a model to follow. They had Sweety. She loved the Lord, went to church, she prayed for her family, she read her word, they watched her work hard all her life. They knew what was right to do. There may have been areas she fell short, but the seeds she planted for the foundation of her family was there. Gerry saw it, he grew from it. The boys just needed the right woman in their life to help their seed grow. Instead they followed a different path without direction to get back.

It's kind of like the parable of the scattered seed in Matthew 13. Some seed fell on the pathway, the birds came and ate them. Some fell in shallow soil under some rocks, it grew quickly but died from not having deep roots burned by the sun. Some fell among thorns, it grew but was choked out by those around them. Some fell in good soil and brought forth fruit multiplying for many. I liken Dale to be the one whose seed fell on the ground and was eaten up by those he followed growing up not having a chance to take root. The seed among the rocks is Roman, he was excited, ready to move in the right direction. But without rich support to ground his roots they burnt up and died. Samuel is the seed that grew up among the thorns, he had the word and tried to follow but was choked out by the life he lived and the people he surrounded himself with. Gerry is the seed that fell in good soil. His roots run deep spreading across not only the city of Camden for which he lived, but to places beyond New Jersey helping others following the word of God. It took him to meet people across the country like John Lewis, Hillary Clinton, Barack Obama, Nancy Pelosi, Frank Laut-

Conclusion

enburg, John Edwards, Donald Norcross and more. They continue to feed people today. This is the man of God I married.

As I reflect on all the emotions I have traveled through thus far since Gerry's ascension, I have to ask God to forgive me too. Forgive me for any thought the provision in my life came from ANY source outside of Him. His provision sent the love of Gerry into my life and my love into his. It was His provision that provided the work and financial stability for us our thirty plus years together and for me right now. He is my provider in ALL things. It is His love that has carried me through each day whispering in my ear guiding me every step of the way. Yes, He sees me better than I see and know myself. Thank you Abba. Thank you for giving us thirty plus years of vows we believed in, honored and completed. Each one completed according to Your word, taking one another for better or worse, for richer for poorer, in sickness and in health, to love and to cherish, till death took us apart. We honor You forever. I thank you for giving me a life of purpose, fresh joy and the ability to love greater than before. I said prior God speaks in many ways, we only have to pay attention. In a dream He gave me peace and closure regarding Sweety. In the dream she came to me. She was clear of mind and beautiful as ever. She told me she still loved me and I was her daughter. She also told me she was sorry for what her family did to me. I will always love and miss her as I hold her close in my prayers each night.

It is important to walk in the light. Evil will grow where we allow it. That is why it is so important to plant seeds of love and forgiveness. If we walk in the light, all darkness will be overcome. It can't stand in the same space as light. I won't assume everyone who reads this believes as I do in Jesus Christ as Lord and Savior who came down from heaven and died on the cross to save us and give us eternal life. This is why I wish to give you an opportunity to change your life forever. Christ loves you. We all are sinners worthy of death and hell, but Christ came to change that for us. He wants us to have an abundant life. By receiving Him into our life things will not be perfect, but with Christ living in us He takes over the fight as we walk with Him.

To receive Him is easy as A,B,C. **Acknowledge** that you are a sinner born into this sinful world. You are not alone, we all are. **Believe** Jesus is the son of God who came down from heaven and died for you. He was perfect doing nothing wrong, He loved us so much He stood in our place giving his life in a humiliating death on the cross. **Confess** your sins to Him those you are aware of and those you can not remember. He already knows them but wants to hear you face them for yourself. Then ask Him to take over your life. He will **Receive** you into the body of Christ making you new, reborn; giving a fresh beginning. He is waiting at your heart's door knocking. You just have to open that door and let Him in.

Conclusion

If you have done this, you have just received your salvation in Christ giving you eternal life. You are part of the greatest family there is gaining eternal life. The next step is to meet the church (people) who serve the Lord to surround yourself and grow. Find a faith based, bible believing church with a leader who teaches the word of God. The saved life is not always an easy life but we have power through the Holy Ghost to overcome the battles we face. God bless you, Praise the Lord and WELCOME to the FAMILY!!!

God's Girl

Acknowledgements

There are people who come into and change your life for the better, making you wonder how you ever lived without them. I acknowledge them today with love too deep to truly express.

To my eternal **Pastor Rev. Calvin R. Woods**, my teacher, friend and spiritual father who led me to salvation through Christ giving me knowledge, wisdom and true understanding who Christ is. And in memory of his beautiful wife **Carmen V. Woods** who was my friend, sister and the one who gave me confidence to worship in movement for the Lord. I love and miss you so much.

To my friend and sister in Christ **Bernice Davis**, the appointed angel by God to be the catalyst to Gerry and I meeting, leading to the love and joy that followed. Love you to life sis, I can't thank you enough.

Some come into your life who say they will be there for you no matter what but somehow fade or just go away. Then there are those who stand with you no matter what. Those few are real friends for which I am honored and blessed to have in my life. There are others who have been there not forgotten, but these listed never dimmed their light. I thank all of you for being with me at the worst time of my life and remaining with me during the silence through regular calls, monetary gifts and notes of love. Thank you for still being here with me.

Phillip & Louise Hurtt
Phyllis & James Brathwaite
Tamicka Wyche-Greenidge
Robin Wyche
Joanne Smith Z
Audrey Eubanks
Ronaldlyn Latham
Carol Billa Holmes

Patricia & Alex Jones
Rosann Euele & Reggie Minggia
Julia & Michael Benjamin

Deborah Tavares
M. Suzzette Ortiz
Sherry Smith
Amanda Cordero
Maureen Crumbley

Special Acknowledgements

I'd like to give special thanks and acknowledgement to the **LINCOLN FINANCIAL FIELD, PHILADELPHIA EAGLES FAMILY;** being part of your family was second in Gerry's life after our family. He loved being part of the Eagles Game-Day Staff and Family, Section 109. You made his life rich. Winning the Superbowl was icing on his cake. For that we thank you. And to **Peter Crimmins, WHYY PBS NPR** for the amazing news article telling his story. It meant the world to us.

Thanks to the members of my current church family **THE PERFECTING CHURCH, SEWELL, NEW JERSEY**, where Kevin C. Brown is our Pastor for supporting me in this book as well as my prior collaboration book *Coming Back From Betrayed*. You live what the body of Christ is all about. Love and blessings to you.

Much thanks to **LeeAnn Sims**, my accountability coach who kept me on track to write daily. You're pushing me to stay focused and review daily progress, put my writing in overdrive to complete.

I am truly grateful to you, **Taurea Vision Avant,** the **Queen of Book Profiting** for teaching me there is much more beyond writing my book. I've gained greater insight through your "Vision", masterclass and overall true coaching beyond what I ever imagined.

Finally to my son **KCJ (Kevin)** we may be at a distance today but you are my FIRST born and ONLY son. No matter what, my heart is and will always be filled with love for you.

VIP Supporters

The generous will prosper; those who refresh others will themselves be refreshed. Pr. 11:25NLT Thank you.

LeeAnn Simms - Mickle River, MD
Confidence Coach
Instagram: @leeann.simms
www.leeannwillis.com

Bashawn Moore - Oklahoma City, OK
Editor-Revision Specialist-Artist aka TeacherBay
Instagram: @bmsincere
www.facebook/I.TeacherBay

Dr. Keanna Ralph - Camden, NJ
Consultant Educator her business is Dreamcatcher's International LLC
Instagram: @keannalynette
www.dreamcatchersinternational.com

Verba Brown - Westville, NJ
Business. & Personal Coaching, her business is Designing Your Destiny LLC
Contact: Verba.Brown57@gmail.com

Mimi V West - Camden, NJ
Contractor Owner - WMB Construction Services LLC
Contact: wmbconstructionservices@gmail.com

Angela M Brown - Sewell, NJ
Executive Director, Community Engagement & Strategic Partnerships - Perfecting Ministries
www.theperfectingchurch.org

Sarah Drummond - Gloucester City, NJ
Financial Director with Parkside Business & Community

Joyce Colemon - Waynesboro, VA
Author JJColemon Books

Sherry A Willis - Westampton, NJ
Elder Sherri A Willis - The Perfecting Church

Cynthia Butler - Sicklerville, NJ
Elder - The Perfecting Church

Renee Stephens - Glassboro, NJ
The Perfecting Church

Roseann Euele - Bensalem, PA

Doris Garlic- Sicklerville, NJ

Timika Woolford - Sicklerville, NJ

Sherry Miller - Gambrills, MD

Muriel Davis - Suwanee, GA

About the Author

Baleeia Minggia-Baker, though born overseas, is a South Jersey girl. Baleeia writes the way she speaks, from the heart with integrity and clarity showing compassion for her fellow man. She has been writing for most of her life but only recently became a published author. Baleeia is not only a writer, she's first a worshiper without hesitation in letting you know she's God's Girl. She takes Proverbs 31 seriously as well as the ten talents spoken of in Matthew 25. Her gifts include sewing, baking, making fresh juices, soups, natural skin care creams and healing salves, All these things she enjoys doing to share with others as gifts and on her website along with the word of God. You can't be in her presence without getting some Jesus too. Her home is dedicated to God where she resides as the innkeeper.

Baleeia is a widow still very much in love with her husband Gerry Baker who died suddenly in the early months of the Covid 19 pandemic. She is passionate about her children and grandchildren. Baleeia's faith in God has proven all she has needed, God's hand has provided.

www.ingramcontent.com/pod-product-compliance
Lightning Source LLC
Chambersburg PA
CBHW071435160426
43195CB00013B/1905